Hints for Teaching Success
in Middle School

DATE DUE

3/6/06	
3/21/06	
4/3/06	
4/18/06	
5/2/06	

GAYLORD   PRINTED IN U.S.A.

D1473818

Hints for Teaching Success in Middle School

Robert E. Rubinstein

Illustrations by
James Cloutier

1994
TEACHER IDEAS PRESS
A Division of
Libraries Unlimited, Inc.
Englewood, Colorado

Copyright ©1994 Robert E. Rubinstein
All Rights Reserved
Printed in the United States of America

TEACHER IDEAS PRESS
A Division of
Libraries Unlimited, Inc.
P.O. Box 6633
Englewood, CO 80155-6633
1-800-237-6124

Louisa M. Griffin, *Project Editor*
Diane Hess, *Copy Editor*
Tama Serfoss, *Proofreader*
Wm. H. Long, *Indexer*
Pamela J. Getchell, *Layout*

Library of Congress Cataloging-in-Publication Data

Rubinstein, Robert E.
    Hints for teaching success in middle school / Robert E. Rubinstein; illustrations by James Cloutier.
    xiv, 169 p. 17x25 cm.
    Includes bibliographical references and index.
    ISBN 1-56308-124-5
    1. Middle schools.   2. High school teaching.   I. Title.
LB1623.R83   1994
373.2'36--dc20   94-8902
                                                              CIP

91

We treat and nurture plants and animals according to each one's individual characteristics and needs. Why do we not do the same for our children?

—Bettie Sing Luke
Multicultural Specialist

Contents

Acknowledgments xi

Introduction xiii

1 You As a Teacher 1
  Understanding the Teacher in You 1
  Some Reflections and a Personal Assessment 2
  How Do You Teach? 3
  Multicultural Awareness and Sensitivity 6
    Fostering Cultural Awareness 9
    Exploring the Concept of Multiple Perspectives 12
    The Importance of Mutual Responsibility 13
  References 14

2 In the Classroom 17
  When Students Enter the Classroom 17
  The Room Condition 19
  References 20

3 The Times Teens Live in Today 21
  The Twisted Teen Journey 21
  Teenagers Need Our Respect 24
  The Effect of Today's World on Our Children 27
  References 29

4 Our Students 31
  The Brain 31
  aixelsyD dna ssertS (Mirror-Image This!) 34
  Students at Risk 34
  Student Behavior 35
  The Teacher's Response 38
    Shadowing 39
    "Adopt" a Student 40
    Kid-Focused Staff Meetings 40
    Give Encouragement 41
  References 41

5 Let's Communicate 43
   How Do You Communicate with Students? 43
   On a One-to-One Basis 46
   Positive Discipline 50

6 Teaching! 55
   What We Know 55
   Skills for the Twenty-First Century 58
   Teaching Creativity and Thinking Skills 59
   What Do We Teach and How? 63
   Some Possible In-School Activities 68
      Renaming Students 68
      Telling Tales 69
      Making Masks 69
      Analyzing Pictures 70
      Creating Images 70
      Other Activities 70
   Students in the Community 71
      Mentorships 72
      Community Service 72
   References 74

7 Why Do We Test? 77
   Testing As a Form of Assessment 77
   Preparing Students for a Test 81
   Creating a Test 82
   Teaching Students How to Take Specific Tests 83
      Multiple-Choice Tests 84
      True-or-False Tests 84
      Matching Tests 85
      Fill-in-the-Blanks Tests 85
      Short Answer or Essay Tests 85
      Open-Note Tests 86
      Group Tests 86
      Oral Tests 87
      Student-Created Tests 87
      Projects or Presentations 87
      Interviews 88
      Humor Helps 88

During the Test 89
Scoring Tests 89
Using the Test As a Learning Tool 90
Grades and Evaluations 90
    Portfolios 91
    Goal Sheets 91
    Parent Conferences 92
    Written Progress Reports 92
    Computerized Evaluations 93
References 94

8 **The Positive Parent Connection** 95
Today's Family 97
What Do Parents Want from You? 98
What Do Parents Want for Their Children? 99
The Parent Conference 101
    Before the Meeting 101
    The Meeting 102
Those Difficult Situations 103
Ways to Help Parents Work with Their Kids 106
    Parent Night 106
    Parent Visiting Days 107
    Learning Nights 107
Information Networks for Parents 107
Parents as Volunteers 108
Parents on Steering Committees 110
References 110

9 **Staff Relations** 113
Staff Cohesiveness 113
Personal Conflicts 116
Substitute Teachers 117
Staff Meetings 119
Change 121
The Principal 124
The Teacher-Administrator Relationship 126
References 129

10   **Dealing with Job Stress** 131
     Laughter 131
     Exercise 134
     Self-Awareness 135
     We Are What We Eat—Unfortunately! 136
     The Computer Effect 137
     Self-Defense 137
     Relaxation 138
     References 139

11   **We Are Public Relations!** 141
     Those Studies on Education 143
     The Need to Inform the Public 145
     Ways to Communicate 147
     References 149

12   **Teaching Future Teachers to Teach** 151
     Lack of Educational Innovation 151
     Responsibilities of Colleges of Education 153
     References 155

13   **In the Future** 157
     What We Need to Know 157
     References 160

     Index 161
     About the Author 169

Acknowledgments

The author would like to acknowledge and dedicate this book to good friends and great teachers who have devoted so much of themselves to teaching and helping kids: Christine and Jerry Matsui, Diane Paul, Linda Pennebaker, Stan Turner, Peggy Rubinstein, and to a consistently outstanding and caring Roosevelt Junior High-Middle School staff!

This book is especially dedicated and in memory of Professor Emeritus Charles (Chuck) Reasoner, a wonderful, innovative teacher who had a lot of fun helping me learn!

I would also like to thank Nancy Golden-Guthrie for her advice and expertise; Jim Slemp for his endless resource materials; Bill Kentta for his insights; my editors: Louisa Griffin, Diane Hess, and Suzanne Barchers; and Larry Gold for his advice, concern, and dire warnings.

Introduction

Several years ago, I met one of my former students who had been a member of the nationally known Troupe of Tellers from Roosevelt Middle School, which I originated and still direct. Four years had passed since I had her as a student. She told me that she had just attended three days of lectures, discussions, and workshops for teens at a national church conference. She looked at me and shook her head. "I can hardly remember what any of those workshop leaders said. They just kept speaking at us. It's all a jumble. . . . But," she paused and smiled, "I can still remember nearly every story you told us at Roosevelt!"

I was astonished that she still remembered stories I had told her so long ago and that the stories had such significance for her. Because she showed me how much storytelling meant to her and how effective storytelling could be, I began to look for more opportunities to use stories in all of my classes—personal stories as well as folktales and literature.

Teaching should not be about information, lecturing, testing, and grading. Successful teachers don't teach: They help students learn; they help create success stories. They help students learn to improve, to succeed, and ultimately, to enjoy the experience of learning. They recognize that students are individuals, each living a personal story, each learning in different ways and through a variety of interests. There is no one right way for students to learn. As long as the student does succeed and finds personal enjoyment in education, then the student has achieved the goals of education.

Students do not come to school to fail—to be told they are stupid or can't learn. They do not attend classes to sit through tedious lectures, to be bored, yelled at, disliked, or punished. Why would anyone—student or adult—willingly come to a place for that type of treatment? Our challenge as teachers is to instill in young people excitement, enthusiasm, and a desire to learn, to see the inherent value of learning.

If there is one concept that I would like each of my students to understand, it is that a person cannot achieve success and enjoy life without the help and support of others. I would hope that the student seeks this support and receives it throughout life and, in turn, willingly gives that support and encouragement to others. I would hope the same for every classroom teacher, too.

Hints for Teaching Success in Middle School addresses how we can help students experience success in school and enjoy lifelong learning. Of course, when our students experience success and enjoy learning, we do too. The chapters include discussions on how we teach, on students as teens, and on the various aspects of teaching in schools today. Also included are some practical and focused ideas, thoughts, and activities that teachers can use to help students learn in positive ways. The discussions and information in this book will help the new teacher prepare to teach in today's schools and will also provide the more experienced secondary teacher with insights and motivation for change.

Perhaps you are an experienced teacher who already uses many of these ideas and approaches. That's great! The contents of this book may help you clarify and reinforce your current teaching success and may offer other approaches and reasons for using your techniques to help students learn and succeed.

1

You As a Teacher

It is one of the beautiful compensations of this life, that no person can sincerely help another without helping himself/herself as well.

—Samuel Smiles

UNDERSTANDING THE TEACHER IN YOU

I've been teaching junior high and middle school for the past twenty-four years. During that span, I've seen my teaching philosophy, teaching style, and relationships with my students and with the school staff undergo continual change and, I hope, growth. That's the way it should be.

One of the major understandings I've gained—quite different from what I was told when I attended colleges of education—is that effective teachers do not do "teach," per se. They do not stand in front of a class and pile mounds of information on note-taking students. They do not then require these students to memorize and parrot that information on tests. This simply is not effective learning, or teaching.

Ironically, in our present booming information age, one of the least important educational goals is to teach information. Albert Einstein stated: "Never bother to memorize anything you can look up."

Teachers do need to help, guide, support, and encourage students to learn, to understand how to access and use information, to succeed in school, and, above all, to enjoy learning.

I hope that at the end of each day and with each passing year I can look back at my experience as a teacher and see what I have learned. A teacher must be willing to learn and to model and must be able to change in positive, constructive ways, just as we ask and expect our students to do. I can see where I have done this, and I can see where I have a great deal more learning and changing to do in the coming years to help my students more effectively.

But change is scary. In many ways, change is more frightening to us who teach in self-contained classrooms and often reuse the same convenient and comfortable techniques, textbooks, and materials year after year than it is for the students, who must try to satisfy the expectations of a variety of teachers and, at the same time, learn new skills. How many times do we hear, "Well, it's worked in the past." "If it ain't broke, don't fix it." Both students and teachers feel insecure and frightened in the face of the unfamiliar; they risk failure, confusion, and frustration. Yet these elements are all part of the process of learning and growing. People should be allowed to learn from failure, not be branded with it.

Teaching is not about the past but about the future. Teaching must focus on preparing students to live successfully, socially, and happily in an ever-changing world—in our case, beyond the year 2000. If schools don't develop programs that prepare students for the future, then *we* have failed, not the students.

Studies show that businesses incorporate a new idea within two years and that top businesses allot a significant percentage of their annual budget to the continual training of their employees in new techniques and approaches. All employees undergo this training and are supported by follow-up services. Our schools, though, according to Stephen Glenn (1990) take more than sixteen years to incorporate a new idea. We also know that among the first items to be cut from a tight budget is staff in-service training, which helps us incorporate new ideas into our teaching. Obviously, after sixteen years, any idea is no longer new and may have become irrelevant.

We must commit ourselves to making our best personal and professional effort to effect change, to seek better ways to help students learn to prepare them for the future. But how do we do this? How do we effect such change in learning in our students and in our schools?

We initiate this change by looking at ourselves as teachers. Before students, administrators, schools, programs, parents' attitudes, and public perception can change, we each must take a look at how we teach, how we work toward our goals for students and ourselves, how we relate to our students, and how we can do all of these better.

SOME REFLECTIONS AND A PERSONAL ASSESSMENT

Take a moment to jot down some personal reflections you have about your teaching. For example, list three things you like most about teaching. Then list three things you like least about teaching. (Evaluating papers certainly would be one of these for me!) Go on to list three things you like about yourself as a teacher and three ways you would like to and can improve your teaching. These might focus on technique and might also include personal changes: perhaps relaxing more and enjoying the students as people. Don't be limited by what you can't do or don't have the money for.

At a teacher committee meeting, we were asked to list the attributes of our favorite teachers from our school days. Those attributes most mentioned follow:

- explored ideas and new things
- made what we learned practical and useful
- involved the community and parents
- was off-beat, off-the-wall, did the unexpected
- nurtured us, loved people, acted as our advocates
- was brilliant and wise and sharing
- told us personal experiences, anecdotes, and stories
- was flexible and adaptable
- was so exciting, entertaining, and interesting that we rarely had behavior problems
- was focused
- allowed students to create and have leadership to produce something for themselves
- permitted us to experiment and try new things without being penalized
- never expressed disapproval of students themselves, only of their behavior

In reviewing this list, I was reassured to see how many of these favorite teacher characteristics are pro student and focus on making learning relevant, fun (there's nothing wrong with fun in learning), exciting, and successful for students.

It was interesting and insightful to compare my own views on teaching with what I liked about my favorite teachers. Take a moment and jot down the characteristics of your favorite teacher or teachers. What is your best memory about school? (It may have been lunch—and that's fine, too.) How do you incorporate these characteristics into your own teaching?

You might also ask your students to note characteristics of their favorite teachers and their best memories about school. Then you could take another courageous step: Share your list of characteristics and your memories with the students and ask if they will share theirs.

HOW DO YOU TEACH?

What is your style of teaching? Do you usually lecture? Do you involve the students in learning, or do you give the students directions and expect them to follow through? I recall an anecdote that illustrates one instance of rigid, direct instruction in teaching:

The teacher announced to the class that today they would draw. The boy loved to draw! Why he could draw monsters and buildings and great, long ships with sails.

But the teacher said, "Today we will draw trees." That was okay with the boy. He imagined large, heavy-trunked trees standing firm. Roots reached deep into the earth. The branches soared to the sky with birds flying above. Maybe he'd make it an orange and yellow tree. That would be nice! He began to draw.

But the teacher said, "Don't draw until I say so." She went to the chalkboard. "This is the tree I want you to draw." She drew a skinny, pale brown tree with branches stuck on. The tree looked sick to the boy, but he took out his crayon and drew the skinny brown tree with the stuck-on branches because that was what the teacher said he must do.

And most times when they had drawing, the teacher drew what she wanted them to draw on the board, and the students in class copied the teacher's example.

The following year they had drawing in class, too. When this teacher told them they would do some drawing, the boy didn't imagine anything that he wanted to draw. He waited for the teacher to tell him what he should imagine, what he should draw, and the way it should be drawn . . . but she didn't say any more. And the boy just sat there.

The teacher came over to him and asked, "Why aren't you drawing?"

The boy shrugged his shoulders and answered, "I don't know what to draw. Aren't you going to show us what to draw?"

The teacher smiled. "You can draw whatever you like—any way you like. Go ahead. Use your imagination." And she walked away.

The boy sat there for a while. Then he drew a picture on his paper of a tree, a skinny, pale brown tree with stuck-on branches.

> Children are not things to be molded,
>   but people to be
>   unfolded.
> —Anonymous

Stephen Glenn, who worked with the federal government on educational policy-making during the Carter and Reagan administrations, said that one study showed that 85 percent of students entering school lose 90 percent of their creativity on the first day of school. He noted that before entering kindergarten children possess a great deal of creativity, a desire to explore, and a willingness to take risks and they want to know about all sorts of things. After entering the public school system, they lose that creativity—it's drummed out of them by rules—realizing that if they create and explore, they will probably be punished or labeled. If they don't do what the teacher wants them to do in the way the teacher wants, they fail and feel embarrassed at being different. (Glenn 1990)

Those of us who choose teaching usually do so because we like teaching and we like young people. We also enjoy entertaining and performing in front of a group (in my case, that sometimes means that my captive audience must listen to my terrible puns!). After all, we know we are competing against the mesmerizing TV monster and a fast-paced outside world for the students' attention. "Good teaching is one-fourth preparation and three-fourths theater," stated Gail Godwin, an educator.

We teachers have the most important role in our society and in these children's lives: We have the responsibility of preparing these young people for their future and for our society's future survival. Their futures, their parents, and our society depend on the students' success in school, on how they learn, and on whether they enjoy learning as a beneficial, lifelong process.

Teaching is communication and our society depends on positive, active interpersonal communication for problem-solving. To help young people learn, teachers must be effective, positive communicators. Teachers also need to be quality listeners, to hear what students are saying and *not* saying.

Quality teaching is done with the head, the heart, and the hands. Students learn to think, to feel and share, to be active in school and outside of school. Quality teachers organize, guide learning, and share both successes and failures with the students. Quality teachers understand, have concern for, and try to work with each individual student.

A while ago I attended a meeting on health education. As part of the presentations, a panel of middle school and high school students discussed how they experienced the public school health curriculum and those who taught it. A student panelist offered an opinion that illustrates how we often don't listen to students, or understand how we are not communicating.

These students were discussing the relevancy of the curriculum in the sex education classes taught in our schools. Suddenly, one high school senior stated, "The trouble is that teachers are so concerned with covering all the material from point A to point B that they don't care if we understand it, want to understand it, or if it has any meaning to us. They just keep throwing it out at us. What does this have to do with us? Few teachers allow us to voice our opinions, or interpretations about the material, and discuss our own experiences."

This student's perception scored a direct hit with me. After this, I started to look at my own course curriculum. I realized that in many classes I, too, was obsessed with running my students from point A to point B to cover the course material. But why? To give them a test or grade? To say that we covered and memorized this range of subject matter—whether or not it had any meaning for the students or if they understood it?

I stopped to consider the students who weren't succeeding in my classes and asked myself why? I thought about those who said the class was "too hard" or "too much work." Too often I had dismissed these comments as students being lazy. But perhaps they felt that way because I wasn't involving them enough in the topic or allowing them to contribute, or because I had made the lesson unnecessarily difficult in my zeal to impart information. I made changes in what I taught, how much information I delivered, and in my assignments so that I might better meet the needs of more students. I'm still trying to make changes; some work and some don't.

> It took me all my life to learn to paint like a child.
> —Marc Chagall

Some harmful teacher behaviors include

- rejecting the student and the student's efforts;
- avoiding dealing with a situation or student;
- keeping distant and impersonal;
- patronizing the student or class;
- maintaining rigidity and inflexibility in approach and attitude; and
- blaming or laying guilt on the student.

Some positive and helpful teacher behaviors include

- expecting the student to succeed and do well;
- focusing on identifying the problem (not the person) and how to overcome it;
- taking the time and effort to show personal interest;
- organizing learning so the student will experience success;
- confronting behavior problems and setting goal steps for the student;
- giving the student the responsibility for success; and
- emphasizing the learning process: how to do something rather than just what's produced.

MULTICULTURAL AWARENESS AND SENSITIVITY

Not one of us wants to admit being prejudiced, but each of us is. We prejudge or stereotype according to the way people act, look, dress, speak, or according to their cultural and racial backgrounds. We can't escape our prejudices, but we certainly can be aware of how we react and take measures to counteract those prejudices.

We live and will be living in an increasingly multicultural world, and we must prepare our students to live successfully in such a world. The only way they can do so is to learn about, understand, and appreciate other people's values, heritage, and points of view.

Itzhak Perlman, the wonderful and world-renowned violinist, wrote an article about how people treat those who are physically challenged and how such treatment made him feel. In one incident, hotel staff spoke to the person pushing his wheelchair, but not to him, as if he were deaf because he was paralyzed. This is prejudice.

To insist that a Native-American student look you in the eye when speaking displays cultural ignorance. Many Native-American children are taught *not* to look an adult in the eye because that shows defiance and disrespect.

Schools have been dominated too long by the attitudes, beliefs, and value system of one race and class of people. . . .
We must learn how to tap the rich vein of cultural, ethnic, and racial diversity to improve education for all.

—Gerald J. Pine
"Rx for Racism: Imperatives for America's Schools"

When a teacher returns papers to students with Santa Clauses, Christmas trees, and the like stamped on them; decorates the room with such symbols; or sings religious, proselytizing songs when even one student in the group does not celebrate Christmas, this demonstrates insensitivity and makes that child feel uncomfortable and an outcast. This is either prejudice or just plain ignorance.

Rev. Gregory Flint of the United Church of Christ sent a letter to the Eugene schools and school board regarding Christmas in the schools. His comments included the following:

Please find some consolation and support in the gratitude of other Christians like myself who are grateful for public schools in which no child is alienated because he or she is not a Christian. . . . We have only to look to the ethnic and religious violence of Northern Ireland, Lebanon, India and Eastern Europe to be reminded of what happens when human diversity is not respected. Nor can we forget that the Holocaust was rationalized as a preservation of culture. . . . As a Christian minister, I thank you and the staff for your resolve that the religious integrity of Jewish children, Moslem children, children of all spiritual backgrounds, will be protected in our schools in all seasons. (December 10, 1991, Eugene, Oregon)

Dick Gregory, on one of his album covers, commented on the racial strife between blacks and whites:

Basically Black folks in America do not hate White folks. We hate this stinking white racist system with these stinking white racist institutions, not you. The United States Constitution that gives a man freedom gives you the right to hate me. Individual racism we're not worried about. It's this damn institutionalized racism that's choking us to death. Here's what Black folks is talking about today: a white racist system that keeps me locked in a black ghetto all my life so I've got to develop a different culture to survive with the rats and the roaches. And when I break out and come to your institutions, you ask me the wrong tests. You don't ask me about the ghetto. You ask me about the Eiffel Tower. (Dick Gregory, "The Light Side: The Dark Side," Poppy Industries album, 1969)

As Marian White-Hood noted in her article: "If we are to educate all students, we must first accept them—all skin colors, all hair types, and all face shapes. We must accept their clothing, language, music and dance, and home styles" (1991, 9). If a teacher cannot accept a student as that student comes to class, then how can positive communication be established between teacher and student to help that student learn and enjoy learning? Students can readily sense whether a teacher likes them or not. If not, just as with most people, the walls of defense—anger, defiance, refusal to cooperate—go up as a means of protection and self-preservation.

The following incidents are not fictional and reveal how cultural ignorance actually happened:

- A high school teacher in a class with both white and black students stated that black students were not really Americans.

- A student of color mentioned to her mother that she was never called on in class when she raised her hand. Then she realized that the teacher did not call on any students of color who raised their hands during the entire year.

- A student of color wrestled for the school team for the season. When he was to go to state competition, the coach insisted he get a haircut so he "would look like everyone else" or he would not be allowed to go. His mother asked how her son could look like everyone else unless they peeled his skin off. The principal said there was no reason the boy should be required to get a haircut.

- The Dr. Pepper soda company tried to use its slogan "I'm a Pepper!" in England. However, in England, *pepper* is slang for *prostitute*. The slogan didn't catch on there.

- Chevy spent millions to market its Nova cars in Spain, but no one would buy them there. It would have been helpful to consider the translation. Why would people buy a car that "doesn't go?"

Fostering Cultural Awareness

So we all, students and staff, need to foster cultural awareness. We might do this with a "cultural awareness bulletin board." Each week, a one- or two-page bulletin headed by a statement such as "It is not the custom in India to shake hands" or "Some Native Americans, traditionally, do not cut their hair" might be posted. These will briefly describe some of the beliefs, traditions, current events, feelings, and hurtful experiences that occur as a result of prejudice to a particular ethnic group: For example, Sikhs, Islamic people, specific Asian peoples, elderly people, physically or emotionally challenged people. Leave those bulletins there for a month or more, adding new items each week. This provides some chance to compare cultural attitudes.

The student newspaper should have a "cultural column" devoted to explaining cultural heritage or discussing current cultural issues that may affect students in school or in the community.

According to a U.S. Bureau of Labor Statistics report, in 1989 women made up more than 51 percent of the population in the United States and 45 percent of the workforce. Black Americans were 12 percent of the population; Hispanic Americans, 9 percent; Asian-American, 2 percent; and Native Americans, 0.6 percent. By the next century, we who will have retired will depend on a multicultural, minority workforce to maintain our economy and pay through their earnings and social security for our retirement benefits. Fifty-one percent of the workforce in the United States will be made up of people of color. What happens to us if those people have not learned the skills needed to secure good jobs and survive in our future society?

Equity Newsline outlined obstacles that are discriminatory and that lessen a minority student's opportunities to learn and to succeed in school:

- Many minorities live in poverty with little hope of escaping from this condition.

- Minority students often lack family support for education and family role models who have completed their education.

- Teachers and administrators feel minority students can't succeed.

- Schools track students, labeling them.

- Teachers have little preparation for understanding and teaching minority children and tend to disregard a minority group's views, values, and heritage.

- Teachers and curricula have an overreliance on linear learning and testing.

- Minority children have few role models in school because of a lack of minority teachers and administrators.

- There is not enough school money for minority students' education and for the adequate training of teachers to work with minority students.

- Peer pressure forces minority students to reject school and to drop out of the system.

David S. Martin (1985) noted some aspects of prejudice and ways to reduce it:

- Facts alone are not sufficient to reduce prejudice. Social class prejudice may be stronger than racial or religious prejudice.

- Persons with high self-acceptance tend to have a low degree of prejudice.

- The cognitive, affective, and behavioral components of prejudice are not necessarily related. (You may understand you're being prejudicial, but behave that way anyway.)

- Films and other media can be used effectively to improve attitudes between groups.

- Social contacts between group members may reduce prejudice.

- Amount of time spent learning about a group is directly related to a reduction in prejudice.

- A climate that fosters open discussion of negative feelings can encourage a change to more positive attitudes.

- Understanding the process of prejudice and stereotyping can lead to more accepting attitudes.

Here is a thirty-second way to determine whether a school or teacher values cultural diversity: Just look at the posters, pictures, murals, and bulletin boards in the building or classroom. How many people from different cultural groups are represented and in what ways?

Take some time to check with your students either with a short, private interview or with short written notes to find how you might better meet each one's personal needs. Notes from students may help make the teacher aware that students felt ignored or hurt by some type of treatment by the teacher or others in class, even if such treatment was unintended.

As Patricia Ramsey suggested in her book *Teaching and Learning in a Diverse World* (1987), give your class and yourself this task to do in writing, so you can share the results as a class:

1. When you think of yourself as part of a religious, cultural, economic, or racial group with certain traditions or practices, list the traits or characteristics that identify you as part of this group.

2. Name and explain the importance to you of three family traditions, foods, or objects.

3. In what ways does your family influence your values and points of view?

4. When was the first time you noticed that people were different? How did you feel about that: curious, afraid, interested, angry? Did you ask any adults to tell you why people were different? If so, what did they say?

5. Are there specific people or groups of people who make you feel uncomfortable or afraid? What is it about their looks, dress, the way they act, that makes you feel that way? Do you think you are caught up in stereotyping, or is it reality?

6. When have people discriminated against you? (It may have been just because you were a teenager.) What was the reason for this, and how did you feel and act? What would you have preferred to have happened?

Exploring the Concept of Multiple Perspectives

Take time to look at incidents and concepts from multiple perspectives. Politicians, especially, show us time and time again that a "fact" can be twisted and used to support a wide variety of opposing views. There is no one truth. We must always ask, "Whose truth is this?" We must help our students to learn to question and probe "truths," too.

You might ask students to comment on a newspaper article about a car accident. How would the driver of the car view the accident? What would be the passenger's view? What would be the perspective of the other driver, a policeman at the scene, the family at home, a witness to the accident, the judge in a court trial, and the jury? How would it matter if one or more of these were minority peoples? Exploring one incident can reveal a multitude of perspectives.

Columbus lands, accidentally, in "the new world" and claims he's discovered it. Well, what do the Native Americans think of this? The Vikings? The Marrano Jews who fled persecution and death in medieval Spain by boarding Columbus's ship? How did Columbus's voyage affect our national attitude toward and treatment of Native Americans? (There are no correct answers, only different, equally-valued points of view.) You can have similar discussions about any aspect of history, science, the arts, literature, sports, ethics, and values.

Take a moment to explore the multicultural perspectives of such concepts as love, money, beauty, evolution, music, parent-child relations, school and learning, males and females, death, holidays, and elderly and handicapped people. How would a woman; a teen; a Jewish, Black, or Latino person; a disabled person; and an older person feel about each concept?

It is important, of course, that everyone present, especially the teacher, be open, accepting, and willing to listen without judgment to other people's views. Equally important is that the teacher does not single out a student or students from a particular ethnic group: "Jimmy, you're black. Tell us how you feel." Allow each student to participate on a voluntary basis and as an individual student, not as the representative of the ethnic or minority group in that class.

Have your students look at the media—newspapers, magazines, television— and examine how minorities are represented in news stories, features, cartoons, advertisements, and sitcoms. How do you think a member of the minority group represented would feel about each portrayal? What stereotypes are there?

Several years ago, when my schedule permitted, I taught a twelve-week class that explored cultures: Jewish, Chicano, Black, and Asian. For each culture, we read, discussed, and worked on projects and invited guest speakers on music, religion, storytelling (comparing folktales from different cultures reveals values), prejudice, language (How does the class feel when someone speaks to them in a language they don't understand? How do you think a foreign student who doesn't understand English feels when spoken to in English?), history, and, most important, food—with tastes! We had a great learning experience together!

I hope that we will reach the point when we no longer teach black history during "Black History Month" or women's history during a "Women's History Month," but instead, truly and simply, integrate the significant events and developments of minority peoples as part of our overall look at history—the history of all people trying to live in our world. As one high school student of color noted, "When was the last time you heard the teacher announce, 'Now we will study white history' or 'Now we will study male history'?"

We have Japanese friends who lived in Eugene for nearly six years. The family had to return to live in Japan. In their farewell letter to friends, they wrote:

> Although technology of communication has been tremendously improved, the Pacific Ocean lying between Japan and the United States is huge and vast. Our peoples tend to fill the gap between us with the magic call for 'mutual understanding,' rather than recognizing our differences carefully, which we must first understand. Through our friends and this community, we have been impressed and encouraged to tap into your culture and your society which are almost 180-degrees unsimilar to our own. (June 28, 1993)

We each must learn to recognize, understand, appreciate, and value each culture's differences before we can find the mutual understanding necessary to peacefully and productively coexist and work together for the benefit of all peoples.

The Importance of Mutual Responsibility

Staff members at Roosevelt composed a vision statement for our school as we enter the twenty-first century. The emphasis in this statement is on mutual responsibility. Students, teachers, support staff, and parents all have the responsibility to create a school that is

- a place where all kids are first and none are last;
- a place that excites, challenges, and involves students, staff, and the community;
- a caring school where people relate to each other in a cooperative and collaborative manner;
- a safe place to take risks;
- a place where learning builds around individual student interests;

- a healthy place;
- a place that teaches life skills to enhance personal power and self-esteem;
- a place that teaches through integrated curriculum themes;
- a place where our program dictates time, and time does not dictate our program;
- a multicultural place where we help our community and our world understand, accept, and appreciate our uniqueness as human beings;
- a place where we value our environment through responsible behavior;
- a place where everyone shares in teaching and learning;
- a school whose boundaries extend beyond the physical building. The community offers resources for Roosevelt, and Roosevelt offers resources to the community;
- a school where we recognize parents as partners in the educational process;
- a place where those affected by the decision will be involved in the decision-making process; and
- a place where curricula and programs are boundless and continue to evolve.

REFERENCES

Equity Newsline. Center for National Origin, Race and Sex Equity. 101 S.W. Main St., Suite 500, Portland, OR 97204.

Flint, Rev. Gregory. 1991. Letter to schools, December 10, Eugene, OR.

Glenn, Stephen. 1990. Developing Capable People. Workshop in Portland, Oregon, March.

Gursky, Daniel. 1991. "Warning: Your School May Be Hazardous to Your Health." *Teacher Magazine* (March): 32-36.

Kochakian, Mary Jo. 1992. "Parents Can Set Limits for Teenagers." *Eugene Register-Guard* (July 19): 3C.

Luke, Bettie Sing. 1992. Roosevelt Middle School Multi-Cultural Workshop, June 21-23.

Martin, David S. 1985. "Ethnocentrism Revisited: Another Look at a Persistent Problem." *Social Education* 49, no. 7 (October): 604-9.

Noonan, John F. 1983. "Discussing Racial Topics in Class." *Innovation Abstracts* 5, no. 3 (February).

Pine, Gerald J. 1990. "Rx for Racism: Imperatives for America's Schools." *Phi Delta Kappan* (April): 593-600.

Ramsey, Patricia G. 1987. *Teaching and Learning in a Diverse World.* New York: Teachers College Press.

Roosevelt Middle School Handbook. 1991. Eugene, OR: Roosevelt Middle School.

Rubinstein, Robert E. 1989. "Building an Atmosphere of Success in a Middle School." *Phi Delta Kappan* (December): 328-29.

———. 1986. "Do Schools Discipline Students Too Much?" *Phi Delta Kappan* (April): 614-15.

Slemp, Jim. 1992. "Effective Communication with Kids Takes Practice." *Eugene Register-Guard* (May 10): 2D.

von Oech, Roger. 1986. *A Kick in the Seat of the Pants.* New York: Perennial Library.

White-Hood, Marian. 1991. "An Obligation: Reaffirming Educational Commitments to Minority and At-Risk Youngsters Through Mindful Practice." *Early Adolescence* (July-August): 7-11.

2

In the Classroom

They tell you in school
That you need to learn phonics,
But I tell you
You've got to learn to dance!
—Diane Wolkstein
storyteller and author, at the
National Storytelling Festival '92

WHEN STUDENTS ENTER THE CLASSROOM

Students can pretty well tell what you're like, what learning will be like with you, and how you teach before you ever begin actually teaching. All they have to do is enter your classroom and look around.

When students come to a classroom, they should be able to laugh, wonder, think, feel, and to see color and interesting items around the room. They should understand that learning is exciting and wonderful and fun. In one experiment conducted in 1956 at Brandeis University, researchers found that people's energy and enthusiasm were decidedly affected by the attractiveness of the room in which they were working (Adler, et al. 1992, 196).

Elementary school halls usually have colorful bulletin boards, murals, and student work on display. Yet few secondary schools have such colorful, interesting, vital halls. One of our classrooms at Roosevelt still has huge drawings of some famous faces—Albert Einstein, John Lennon, Anne Frank—on the walls, created by a ninth-grade girl in 1983. Each time I have the chance to see these drawings I'm awed by the tremendous talent she has, and the legacy she left to us through these works of art. Who wants to look at pale green walls when they can have rainbows and scenes of mountains before them? There should be murals—especially ones showing teen life and interests—painted by teens. Why don't students have a chance to put up more posters and bulletin boards in the halls, the cafeteria, the library, and in student activity rooms? Each hallway should have a permanent banner stating: This is your school, your future, . . . your life!"

I try to find a special poster for the window of my classroom door. Sometimes it's humorous and features animals, but more important, it usually says something about sensitivity and positive, caring relationships—a message I would like students to carry with them across the threshold of my classroom.

Beyond the classroom door it's all color and variety! I have posters of sports figures on the walls. (Do you know how difficult it is to find sports posters of famous women athletes?) Also on the rainbow-striped walls, I have posters of scenes, sayings, animals, movie actors, foreign lands, imaginings, and things to make one wonder.

My other room decorating usually follows a pattern:

1. One bulletin board advertises a class I'm teaching or a class I will be teaching next term if registration for the next term is approaching.

2. Another bulletin board focuses on humor, either general with cartoons and writings or devoted to *Far Side*, *Peanuts*, or another cartoon.

3. The third bulletin board focuses on contemporary life and happenings: usually a "What in the World!" or a "Teen Life!" board. In the classroom, I do not want to express just my own interests, but also what I feel teens will find interesting, funny, startling, and sensitive. And I want to do this in whatever way will make my room an exciting, colorful, and fun place to learn. Students also can contribute to these boards.

All during the year, I then use these posters and bulletin board displays. I can use them for assignments:

• Choose a scene shown in the room and describe it in detail. Who do you think lives there? What type of world is it?

• Find a character—real or imaginary, human, animal, or other—and describe that character's family life, hopes, and dreams.

• Explain, in writing or orally, what you find funny in one of these cartoons or situations.

• Act out one of the scenes and/or characters you see on the walls.

You don't have to be an artist to create some appealing bulletin boards. With the advent of the copy machine, especially the color copier, illustrations can be adapted to the board you would like to create. If you copy photos of famous people or of historical events, include a brief note about who these people were/are or the time, place, and importance of the event. Collect old issues of *Newsweek*, *Sports Illustrated*, *Reader's Digest* (for the jokes, the vocabulary word lists, and the wonderful "Personal Glimpses" page) and other magazines to provide pictures and articles for your displays. If you teach classes such as mythology, movies, sports, biographies, music theater, or monsters, the library has a wide range of books with anecdotes and photos to use.

Many computer programs also include graphics components. Computer-generated graphics can be used to create bulletin board illustrations. Computers usually have lettering capabilities also, allowing you to make titles and banners. If for some reason you do not have access to these computer programs, ask for a volunteer. Often an aide, secretary, parent, or student has a special skill in designing and lettering.

THE ROOM CONDITION

When students sit in deep rows, the teacher can't see all the students, and they can't all see the teacher or the board; students in the back may not be able to hear as well. Such situations often lead to lack of attention and behavior problems, the "lost back row" syndrome.

These past years, I've had three rows spanning the length of my room and facing the blackboard. This allows me to maintain eye contact with nearly every student, and vice versa. When I've taught discussion classes, such as a personal communication class, I've chosen a circle or semicircle arrangement, which gives each student contact with every other student in class. This helps promote direct, sensitive personal communication.

Desks act as a physical barrier that separates the teacher from the students. (One study done with doctors demonstrated that simply removing the doctor's desk as a barrier between doctor and patient made the patient feel nearly five times more at ease during office visits [Adler, et al. 1992, 198].) You want to be able to walk in front of your students, among them, behind them. I want to be able to sit on a desk with them to talk more intimately at times. Try to structure the room so you have this flexibility and can change focus and feeling while teaching.

Do you have flexible seating? Are chairs and desks separate and movable so students can form groups for cooperative learning or move to long tables to work on a project?

I must have been teaching three or four years in the same classroom before I consciously walked to different parts of the room to look at the blackboards. I suddenly realized—it should have happened long before—that from different parts of the room, students could not read the blackboards because of the glare from outside or poor lighting in the room itself. This glare changed depending on the time of day and on the blackboard I used.

So I tried to make certain that I read aloud whatever I wrote on the board. If a student asked me to read it again, I did. Often, I encourage students to leave their seats and move to the front of the room to copy the board information and then return to their seats. I have also changed from white to yellow chalk.

The lighting in the room itself is an important factor for learning and concentration. When I was a children's librarian in the South Boston Public Library, Martha Engler and I would travel out to the South Boston schools to tell stories and give booktalks. The old schools there had terrible lighting. I had difficulty just reading selections from the books I presented. The lighting hurt my eyes and made me feel tired. How could those children read for any extended period of time under those conditions? Even today, most schools pay little attention to the effect lighting has on students' eyes, attention, and energy.

What kinds of noises are there in your room and around your room? For years, the heating system in my room would start to bang so loudly that at times I had to take the students from the room because we couldn't hear each other and they couldn't concentrate on reading. By the end of these days, I would have a tremendous headache and be short-tempered. (The superintendent came once to observe class and the radiator started banging. She left and said how terrible it was, that no one could teach under those circumstances, and something should be done about it.) Noise can produce elevated pulse rates, headaches, rapid heartbeats, stress, and distraction.

Do you have good air circulation in the room? Teachers in a school in Hartford, Connecticut, for example, complained of the lack of fresh air in the classrooms. They proved that this lack of fresh air caused teachers to suffer from headaches, dizziness, and fatigue. If teachers suffer this from a lack of fresh air, then wouldn't children also suffer at least as much or more? These conditions lead to dramatic mood swings, an inability to concentrate, and a feeling of extreme weariness in many children. Who can learn under these conditions?

A lack of well-circulated air also allows pollutants to gather and cause health problems. A 1991 article by Daniel Gursky in *Teacher Magazine* stated: "Health experts believe that indoor air pollution presents one of the country's largest public health hazards. By some estimates, indoor pollutants cause more than half of all minor illnesses" (36).

REFERENCES

Adler, Ronald B., Lawrence B. Rosenfeld, and Neil Towne. 1992. *Interplay: The Process of Interpersonal Communications.* New York: Harcourt Brace Jovanovich College Publishers.

Gursky, Daniel. 1991. "Warning: Your School May Be Hazardous to Your Health." *Teacher Magazine* (March): 32-36.

Lee, Renee. 1992. "Study Finds Poor Classroom Air Quality." *Eugene Register-Guard* (May 18): 1C.

3

The Times Teens Live in Today

This is America's opportunity to help bridge the gulf between the haves and the have-nots. The question is whether America will do it. There is nothing new about poverty. What is new is that we now have the techniques and the resources to get rid of poverty. The real question is whether we have the will.
—Dr. Martin Luther King, Jr.
March 1968

THE TWISTED TEEN JOURNEY

When we adults think of teenagers, we often see the oddities: the raging and quick-changing emotions; the hormones; the questioning and challenges; the strange clothes, hairdos, music, language. We feel distant and alienated from these young people, puzzled, and sometimes scared. And we forget.

We forget that this story has played and replayed throughout history: There is a time to leave childhood behind and to undertake the journey to adulthood. Every generation, every culture, has recognized the journey, ritualized this evolution, and celebrated the new person's emergence from the cocoon. We would more readily understand and accept this if we still had families, especially extended families, intact and if our rituals still had significant substance and meaning—if we paid more attention to and had more respect for the traditional folktales and values that tell us about the importance of this journey.

But we don't. Instead we try to minimize this journey, ignore the changes as much as possible, and separate our adult selves from teen life. We forget, too, that no such people as "teenagers" as a social group existed in our society before 1945, or in other nations of the world. The son of a farmer worked the fields

as a man at the age of twelve. The twelve- and thirteen-year-old girls I met as a volunteer in the mountains of Mexico would marry and bear children within the next year or two of their young lives. They understood that they would experience the traditional struggle of life.

However, in the affluent United States, and now in most of the affluent industrialized world, we have arbitrarily decided that these young people, who at the ages of twelve or fourteen are biologically adults and who, throughout history, have participated in the adult world, cannot do so today. They must remain arrested in their journey of natural human evolution in a stage called "teenager."

We insist that they suspend their biological readiness, that they suspend their participation in adult society until they graduate from college, maybe graduate school, because our highly industrialized and technological society has no place for them. They should not have children until they can "afford" them, so they now must wait until their late twenties or early thirties to begin families. And we expect and demand that they somehow restrict their sexual activity, too. Then we wonder why teens "have problems," seem antisocial, uncooperative, and destructive.

We keep delaying the journey, dangling these young people in a suspended life process. The young hero must leave home, but we have no place for the hero to journey to, no goal in sight. The journey, as David Oldfield notes in "The Adolescent Crisis: The Hero's Journey," is a quest for power. Teens search for a way to be in control of their own lives, to choose their own paths, to feel valued by others. We don't permit this to happen. The traditional tale allows the hero to recognize that he or she is ultimately responsible for what happens on this life journey, for decisions made and their consequences. We don't allow this to occur. We often don't assist and encourage these young people in beginning and following through on this journey, and yet their journey today is far more difficult than at any time in history.

> Today the matter is much more complex, for the battles engaged in
> by modern adolescents are primarily internal and emotional rather
> than external and physical. Issues of identity, self-worth, developing
> a set of personal values and meaningful goals to strive toward: these
> are the skirmishes for which our contemporary heroes must be
> equipped. (Oldfield 1991, 31)

Yet in 1988, 90 percent of teen suicides (suicide is the second leading cause of death among teenagers) stemmed from feelings of not being valued, needed, listened to, or taken seriously. The same feelings lead to many, over a million per year, teens becoming mothers (Glenn 1990). Mothers have control; young children must listen to mothers. So these young people do receive our adult message: "You're the future. You're important to us. However, don't show up until *we* need you and *we* call."

I'm the child with no direction,
No place to run and nowhere to go;
They've branded me defiant and sometimes
Call me slow.

I'm the one that love forgot, care abandoned
And hope took leave.
Seems I don't have much of a future—
Is that so hard for you to believe?

———Julie Ellis (White-Hood 1991)

If we look deeper at the structure of the folktale motif of the hero's journey we see that the hero often fails. Failure is expected, necessary, to learn about choices and consequences. If there are three brothers, the first two brothers usually fail to accomplish the task, or suffer grave repercussions because of their choices (more often due to behavior or values rather than to lack of skills). The young hero learns from these failures and adjusts so that he can achieve success, happiness, good fortune, and peace. Our traditional school curriculum, though— the way we teach and the way students must learn—doesn't allow for failure or emphasize the value of failure, the important learning that can be gained from a failure. Condemnation accompanies failure based on lack of skill development without consideration of the student's attitude, behavior, and value choices.

The Chinese word for *crisis* is made up of two characters. The first character stands for *danger*. The second character means *opportunity*. Young people must be allowed to look for opportunities and to take risks without our punishing them, and must be allowed to work toward their personal growth goals.

TEENAGERS NEED OUR RESPECT

Over 90 percent of humans are "other-related." They function or do not function depending upon and responding to how others see them. Ten percent are so-called supernormals. These are the healthiest people; they have a sense of self and have personal satisfaction from within (babies usually have these characteristics) (Glenn 1991). We can readily see the influence of peers on "other-related" teens. We can understand the devastating effects when peers turn against a young person.

Teenagers should have some rights and considerations as people who are experiencing an important and decisive time of their lives—transition to adulthood and to becoming contributing members of our society. Teenagers are in transition; they are not full adults and no longer children. Teenagers should:

- have some time to play, relax, and be with friends. Socialization is an important part of growing up.
- be shown love. They need to be liked and appreciated as people and allowed to give love and appreciation in return.
- have privacy. Struggling as they are to determine who they are, what to think, and how to act, teens need their privacy; they need to have private thoughts and belongings. We should respect this need except when they seem to be in imminent danger.
- have a right to express personal opinions and not be penalized because those opinions may differ from others.
- have a right to be treated fairly, and to have a fair hearing before any guilt or punishment is determined.

The following would be an interesting exercise to compare the differences in generations of young people. List these topics on the board:

Family life

Adult jobs

School (subjects taught, atmosphere, teachers)

Cost of things (milk, movies, ice cream, gasoline, etc.)

Types of movies

Types of stress

People's concerns

Drugs of choice

Types of physical conflicts

What people expect or expected in the future

(Hallmark's "Birthday Times" and other variations of greeting cards list the events and costs of items during specific years. These could be used for discussion.)

These question sheets can be given to students, the teacher, and other adults, including senior citizens, to complete. Those answering these questions can write word groups or phrases; they don't have to write sentences. After the responses are completed, break into small groups and discuss the answers. Try to come to some agreement and note the differences, especially in generations. From here, have a discussion with the entire group. Senior citizens might tend to comment on the changes they've seen. It's not only important to note the changes from one generation to another, but also vital to discuss why these changes have occurred and the implications for the future. Often, the predominant question teens have while trying to exist in the larger, more anonymous middle schools is whether life is really worth living. If we want them to answer this question with "Yes, life is worth living," then we must find the ways and time to give them the personal attention and support they need to grow up as healthy people in both body and mind. Support must come before challenge to help young people grow.

The most critical need for any person is to find meaning, purpose, and significance. In order to do this, that person must feel understood, accepted, and affirmed.

According to Abraham Maslow, any person has *basic needs* that must be met before that person can progress in individual growth and ultimately reach the goal of *self-actualization* (truth, goodness, and beauty). These basic needs are progressive—the person must obtain them in an orderly fashion. The most basic needs are *physiological* ones and ones that concern *safety and security*. The physiological needs are air, food, water, shelter, and sleep. The safety and security needs are personal, social, and global. These needs must be met before one can move up to the next level.

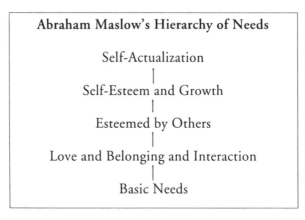

Abraham Maslow's Hierarchy of Needs

Self-Actualization
|
Self-Esteem and Growth
|
Esteemed by Others
|
Love and Belonging and Interaction
|
Basic Needs

There are other types of needs, however. *Growth needs* do not necessarily progress in this step-by-step direction and may be reached in many different ways and in random order. Growth needs include aliveness, individuality, perfection, necessity, justice, order, simplicity, richness, playfulness, effortlessness, self-sufficiency, and meaningfulness.

Teachers should study the implications these hierarchies have for a student's readiness and ability to focus on learning and succeeding in school.

THE EFFECT OF TODAY'S WORLD ON OUR CHILDREN

According to statistics, the American home has become a place more dangerous for children than even the city streets. The National Center for Child Abuse noted that

- there are 2.5 million cases of child abuse reported each year;
- more than 95,000 children commit suicide annually;
- a twelve-year-old child had a better chance in 1935 of reaching the age of twenty-five in good health than a twelve-year-old child does now; and
- every day in the United States we bury over 1,000 twelve- to twenty-three year-olds needlessly. That's ten times more teens dying each day than American soldiers who died in the entire Persian Gulf War! As a nation, we mourned and recognized the deaths of these soldiers but do basically nothing about our dying youth (Glenn 1991).

Today, children return to empty houses or no houses at all, not enough food, abuse, single and stressed-out parents, and little supervision and support. They carry knives and guns, even to school, for protection because they're afraid. This plight of our children crosses socioeconomic lines from the rich to the very poor.

We have developed a country that leads the industrialized nations of the world in violence, crime, teen pregnancy, child abuse, and drug and alcohol abuse. Other nations of the world, for the most part, maintain their steady support of public education, realizing their children hold the key to the world's survival. In our country, we undermine education with tax limitation measures, closure of colleges of education, and constant public and federal censure (often politically slanted) of nearly every aspect of public education.

Dr. D. Stanley Eitzen, professor of sociology at Colorado State University, stated, "My strong conviction is that children are *not* born with sociopathic tendencies: problem children are socially created. . . . We must understand this sociocultural context of social problems in order to understand problem students and what we might do to help them" (1992, 585-86). Dr. Eitzen also notes the dramatic changes and forecasts for our social, political, and economic future. No longer can we pretend we are an independent nation, the nation that has the strength to stand alone. Now we must survive in a global economy; we must understand how and why other nations and people act. Yet within our own society, racial and ethnic conflict and violence keep increasing, revealing our inherent lack of understanding and ability to change.

Industries have collapsed; capital investment is short-term; the shift is toward high-tech and service-based industries. Many of these new jobs have lower pay and fewer benefits. By 1986, the cost of sending one child to a private college was over 40 percent of the average family's income, typically with both parents working. The Reagan-Bush years and policies dramatically increased the income gap between the richest 20 percent and the poorest 20 percent of Americans to the greatest gap ever recorded in our nation's history.

As a result of all these factors, teens today can expect to be the first generation that will have a lower standard of living than their parents. In 1992, the National Scholastic Survey's "Teen Sting," conducted in high schools in thirty-seven states, found that 50 percent of teens said their families had been affected by recession, 33 percent knew someone who had lost a job due to recession, 66 percent were not learning about recession in school, and 50 percent did not understand economic issues or what caused recession (26).

Fred M. Hechinger in *Fateful Choices* (1991) pointed out that in this decade the state of adolescent health has reached crisis proportions in both breadth and depth. Due to depression, thousands of teens commit suicide; thousands more abuse themselves with alcohol (which our government refuses to seriously control) and illegal drugs. Then there are the many thousands who risk AIDS with unprotected sexual activity, lack adequate nutrition and exercise, and become the victims or causes of violence. The stress and insecurity teens experience often overwhelm them. More than 8 million American adolescents, that's about 27 percent of them, live in poverty or near poverty-level conditions. Illness becomes a monumental financial problem for them and their families, because more than 15 percent have no medical insurance of any sort.

More than 20 million young people participate in nonschool sports, both recreational and competitive, resulting in lifelong injuries or bodily traumas such as arthritis, tissue tears, and damaged bone growth. The barrage of activities—sports and others—inundates young people. Some young people are on the run from six or seven in the morning until seven or eight at night without a chance to rest, and their activities don't necessarily decrease on weekends. Such a schedule becomes more of a punishment than any fun; children often endure the schedule so as not to disappoint their parents. They have no time to relax and be children. Dr. Sheila Ribordy, the director of clinical psychology training at De Paul University, related, "One eighth-grader I know broke down crying in front of her mother and said she couldn't take the pressure anymore. She asked her mother, 'Why do you always think there's something wrong if I want to stay home and be by myself?' " (Kutner 1992, 2F).

Only 28 percent of young people read for fun at home, and they read fewer newspapers and magazines today than they did in 1984. Most of their news and life information comes, of course, from television. Much of this information, however, is highly slanted and censored, depending on who selects the information that's presented. In today's world, according to an Educational Testing Service study—"America's Smallest Schools: The Family"—the United States ranks second among all other nations in the percentage of thirteen-year-olds who watch at least five hours of television each day, and seemingly as a result, these American students rank second from last in mathematical skills. This study concludes with the observation that "change must occur in the pervasive attitude of American society—and this change must begin with the family. National education goals for the year 2000 will be difficult to attain without educational reform in the home as well as in the school" ("A Shaky Foundation" 1992, 29).

REFERENCES

Child Help U.S.A. "National Child Abuse Statistics." Box 630, Hollywood, CA 90028.

Eitzen, D. Stanley. 1992. "Problem Students: The Sociocultural Roots." *Phi Delta Kappan* (April): 584-90.

Glenn, Stephen. 1991. "Changing Paradigms for Youth" workshop. Eugene, OR, October 11.

———. 1990. "Developing Capable People" workshop, Portland, OR, March.

Hechinger, Fred M. 1991. *Fateful Choices.* New York: Carnegie Corporation of New York.

Kutner, Lawrence. 1992. "Full Schedules Stress Youngsters." *Eugene Register-Guard* (November 15): 2F.

Lippman, John. 1992. "TV's Changed How We View World Culture." *Eugene Register-Guard* (October 25): 3A.

Maslow, Abraham. "Hierarchy of Needs."

Micheli, Lyle J. 1990. "Children and Sports." *Newsweek* (October 29): 12.

National Scholastic Survey. "Teen Sting." 1992. *NEA Today* (November): 26.

Oldfield, David. 1991. "The Adolescent Crisis: The Hero's Journey." *Early Adolescence* (July-August): 28-35.

"A Shaky Foundation for Learning." *NEA Today* (November 1992): 29.

Slemp, Jim. 1989. "From the Principal." *Roosevelt Middle School Community Newsletter* (November): 2.

White-Hood, Marian. 1991. "An Obligation: Reaffirming Educational Commitments to Minority and At-Risk Youngsters Through Mindful Practice." In *Early Adolescence* (July/August): 7.

Our Students

> *There is no good to be gotten from consistently pointing out a person's shortcomings. We need to find and encourage every person's individual competencies. That is our job. That is why we are teachers.*
>
> —Ruth Ann Blynt
> "The Sticking Place: Another Look at Grades and Grading"

Before we attempt to help and guide students to learn successfully, we should try to keep in mind some major understandings about how people learn.

THE BRAIN

As teachers, we do not teach students to think. Studies show that from birth, perhaps earlier, the human brain thinks. What we can do is help students access and use their natural ability to think and help them learn to organize.

According to David Sousa's research on brain activity and learning, our senses provide more than 40,000 bits of information *per second*. Our brains filter this information, deciding what is important and what is not. The brain makes decisions in milliseconds about these information bits. What a student hears a teacher say in class is only a fraction of the information bits bombarding his or her mind each second.

We have two main types of memory: working memory and long-term memory. The functioning of our working memories depends on our ages. Students fourteen years of age and younger have a working memory with an attention span of *five to ten minutes*. The over-fourteen-year-old person has a working memory with an attention span of *ten to twenty minutes*.

Once a person has reached the limit of his or her normal attention span, any more time on the same task becomes a battle with mental fatigue. What happens, then, when students must sit through a forty-five-minute or an

hour-plus class, often doing the same task or being forced to sit and listen to a lecture? What implications does this fact have for behavior and cooperation problems with students?

Information either passes from the working memory to long-term storage or it is discarded. The student will retain information if it seems important, has meaning, or makes sense to the student. The student determines the value and meaning of information based on past experience. If past experience has been largely negative, this will color what seems important or relevant and the attitude toward the information stored. ("This is garbage, but I have to remember it for a while to get through this class.") Past learning experiences then affect new learning. ("This is all garbage that has no use for me—so why should I learn more on my own?")

In their 1990 article "Understanding a Brain-Based Approach to Learning and Teaching," R. Caine and G. Caine noted that learning is a process that engages the whole human body, and that a person's physiological development affects the capacity and readiness to learn. All young people do not have the same brain development or physiological development at any specific age or stage in their lives. So why do we place so much emphasis on national measurements and standardized tests—in the process causing young people so much stress—to determine students' capabilities and futures? Each student develops at his or her own pace, according to a physiological readiness that is not necessarily of that student's choosing.

The Caines also found that emotion and learning cannot be separated. The brain responds much more positively to challenges when the learner is not threatened or put under stress. Classrooms that have positive, relaxed atmospheres promote much more successful learning experiences than do rigidly controlled classrooms with students consistently suppressed, regimented, and tested.

We need to remind ourselves that students remember

- 10 percent of what they read,

- 20 percent of what they hear,

- 30 percent of what they see,

- 50 percent of what they see and hear,

- 70 percent of what they discuss with others,

- 80 percent of what they experience by doing,

- 95 percent of what they teach to others.

("Weekly Staff Bulletin," Roosevelt Middle School, March 13, 1992)

These statistics only reflect what has been observed before. A Chinese proverb states, "What I hear I forget. What I see I remember. What I do I understand," and a Japanese proverb recognizes that "To teach is to learn."

This is why, as Stephen Glenn pointed out, the most effective school we have ever had is the one-room schoolhouse. Here the teacher knew and worked with each student individually. The older students had the responsibility of helping the younger ones in class. This allowed for bonding and understanding. As a result, graduates from these schools—some of these schools are in the Dakotas even today—showed 600 percent more initiative and capability than those students in large classes using standardized curriculums. A much larger percentage of these one-room schoolhouse students went on to college and received scholarships than did students from traditional public schools.

AIXELSYD DNA SSERTS (Mirror-Image This!)

Thomas Edison and Albert Einstein never did very well in school, yet they are acknowledged geniuses. They did not do well in school because both had dyslexia, a learning disability caused by some type of brain misfunction. According to research, most of those who are dyslexic have average or above-average intelligence, they often see printed words backward, upside down, or reversed. Nearly one out of ten students in school has some degree of dyslexia, which affects reading; writing, especially spelling; and self-confidence. Often, these students find themselves in remedial or special education classes, labeled, perhaps, for the rest of their school lives.

In a more general sense, a learning disability can affect how a student receives information, interprets that information, and files it in long-term memory. The person may have a problem with retrieving and using that information from memory. Each person's learning ability or disability is unique.

Teachers should be more alert to such disabilities. They should consider ways to help those who, for example, have great difficulty with spelling, rather than penalizing students for that disability and, in so doing, producing more frustration and failure. A teacher with dyslexia recalls that "spelling has always been very traumatic for me. Usually I know the letters but not the order."

STUDENTS AT RISK

Today, almost all students are "at-risk." Only about 20 percent to 30 percent of students in our schools do *not* receive some type of special service. Approximately 70 percent of the students in a classroom come from divorced families, stepfamilies, or single-parent situations. All of these situations have dramatic effects on students' self-confidence, sense of security, belief in adult support, ability to concentrate, and attitude toward life and learning.

The single biggest factor with these at-risk students, according to Nancy Golden, nationally known expert and director of educational services for Eugene schools, is absenteeism. The main antidote for this is attention: personal, caring adult attention. Stephen Glenn, in his "Developing Capable People" workshop, said, "Consider the irony. Today's children will be forced to accept more years of education than most people in history could only have dreamed of having. And to many of our young people today, education seems like a curse" (1990). Following are some of the obstacles to student success:

- preacademic records that fail to recognize that students learn at different rates;

- tracking, prior labeling, and placement that imprison a student in an environment where expectations are that the student will never succeed;

- a low socioeconomic level of the family that precludes their providing the necessary support services;

- judgments based on physical appearance;

- judgments based on verbal expression (language ability supposedly reflects the student's intelligence and capability because that student has learned to speak according to the accepted norm); and

- gender and race barriers and assumptions that trigger expectations, negative and positive, about that student's attitude, capabilities, and direction.

A Carnegie Council on Adolescent Development workshop observed that

young adolescents have a great need for intimacy, yet we put them in large, impersonal schools. Young adolescents need increased autonomy and they need to make their own decisions, yet we put them in environments of review and rote learning. Young adolescents show great variability among themselves and within themselves, yet we put them in classrooms where we ignore their variability and need for flexibility. (1989)

STUDENT BEHAVIOR

In their passage from childhood to adulthood, teens have two very important concerns. One is how to assert themselves—to express what they need and how they feel as young adults. The other is how to shift goals and adjust to new situations without losing self-confidence and suffering ridicule. The only way they can proceed is by testing different—sometimes manipulative—behaviors to see what happens.

If students are allowed to use manipulative behavior at will and without consequences, they will probably do so as adults, alienating others. However, if adults react too heavily to such behaviors and social skills, then the student will likely have problems in the adult world, where people often do use manipulation— a catch-22 for both students and teachers. The teacher has to determine when such behavior should be allowed and when it has gone too far.

Experienced teachers, as Jim Slemp, principal of Roosevelt Middle School, pointed out, know these behavior games:

- divide and conquer. The student pits one teacher against another. Both teachers and the student need to meet and clarify the situation.

- "Everyone else gets to." The student attempts to make the teacher feel guilty. ("Everyone else gets to go outside. Why won't you let us?") The student should be made aware that teachers make decisions on an individual basis. (There's always the "Brooklyn Bridge" analogy!)

- "I know what I'm doing." This is the student's bid for independence, for not constantly being told what to do. The teacher could try explaining the consequences beforehand and then allow the student to proceed in his or her own way as a practical learning experience.

- "Up yours!" This is a teen's way of cutting off communication by using offensive remarks. The challenge is to keep calm and not respond with similar exclamations and attitude.

- "I win, you lose!" The student is keeping score in an attempt to make communication a contest between teen and adult power. The key is to find ways and to show the student that you both can win or you both lose. We learn together. (1990, 2)

In the "Fresh Voices" section of *Parade* magazine, Lynn Minton (1992) focused on ways for parents to get along better with their kids. Many of these "rules," as suggested by kids, could be used by teachers to get along better with their students:

- "Listen carefully to me." (David Farwell)

- "Listen before you yell." (Tom Philpot)

- "Even though our problems may seem ridiculous to you at times, don't tell us to forget it. Give us advice." (Meg Bustaque)

- "Lighten up a little." (Allison Miller)

- "Be honest with me." (paraphrased)

- "Show a little happiness." (Josi Smucker)

Rottier, Stone, and Kinka (1988) of the University of Wisconsin emphasized in their video "Early Adolescence—A Time for Change: Implications for the Family" that normal behavior for a teenager will often appear strange to us. They suggest responses to these behaviors and reasons for them:

- If a student is caught up in idealism, work with that child to understand that anyone can make a mistake. More realistic expectations of self and of others help ease stress and disillusionment.

- Brain growth slows down during these years, largely due to the onslaught of all the hormonal changes. There will be fluctuations in the quality of work and in attention spans. Tasks should be broken into smaller, well-defined steps. (I remember several years ago one teacher assigned an in-depth book report to be completed six weeks hence. She gave no other instructions and did not provide checkpoints for the students to see how they were doing or if they understood what to do. Then she wondered why so few completed the assignment and why others didn't meet her expectations.)

- Behaviors will vary from childlike to adult without discernible cause or justification. This is part of the process of intellectual maturing. This process doesn't move ahead on a straight path; little in life does. Discussions on values and perceptions and including the student in decision-making help.

An article in *Phi Delta Kappan* pointed out that students' feelings about school depend on their perceptions of how they are treated and on their success. There's a strong desire to be recognized as a person, an individual, not just as a member of the class. "In classrooms where personalities are allowed to show, students respond more fully, both academically and personally" (Phelan, Davidson, and Cao 1992, 696). This article also mentioned that students appreciate a well-organized and orderly classroom atmosphere, but they do not enjoy one in which the teacher appears detached, not interested in their individual learning and understanding. Having classes with friends holds great importance, because students then are with people they know, can trust, and can rely upon for help. Students are more willing to participate in a class in which they know a lot of the people.

Students like to be challenged, not tricked. However, they do not like teachers or classmates who ridicule them or make them feel stupid. Why would anyone risk further participation under these circumstances? (I still remember the pompous teacher in senior honors English who purposely tried to embarrass me in front of the class by bombarding me with spelling words. He knew I had difficulty spelling. He wanted to use me as an example to show how much the class needed to study for the spelling test. Ten years later, when I found out he still was teaching, I relished returning to his class with my masters degree in English, nationally published articles, and accomplishments as a storyteller!)

High-achieving students want a teacher to offer academic assistance; students who are lower achievers value more person-to-person teacher help, and attention that may go beyond just the academic. Such a student values a teacher with patience, a sense of humor, the ability to listen, and the willingness to help. When these students sense that a teacher doesn't really care about them personally, they lack the incentive to do their work or to participate. They learn from the teacher, with the teacher's help, and, as studies show, accomplish much less from textbook reading and work. "Some kids don't know that they want to learn until you put it in their heads that they do" (Kidder 1989, 285).

THE TEACHER'S RESPONSE

After teaching for over twenty years in the same school, I now have children whose parents were once my students. I've also taught several children from the same family. (One family has had four children in my storytelling troupe, spanning a fourteen-year period. I think it's become a family expectation and tradition to perform in the troupe.) I have to constantly alert myself to *not* compare one child to a sibling. Each student has a right to be accepted and treated as an individual, as free as possible of prejudicial judgments based on other family members. (As it is, I often call one by the other's name—and receive, rightfully so, disgusted looks in response.)

Each student is unique in experiences, views of life, capabilities, and weaknesses. That student is not responsible for what a brother or sister, a mother or father, did or did not do and should not have to carry the burden of expectations based on other family members' accomplishments.

We should convey to each student that we value his or her special capabilities or talents. Whatever a brother or sister did was fine, but we like this person for himself or herself. For the student to develop a healthy, accepting self-view, the teacher must offer sincere encouragement and praise.

When a student doesn't do the work, behaves disruptively, refuses to cooperate, gets in trouble, the teacher should find ways to allow the student to rebuild trust. Distrust only breeds more distrust, anger, and tension ("When is he going to do it again?" "She thinks I'm bad anyway, so I might as well be.") for both parties.

Assuming the teacher is not dealing with drugs, serious crime, or potential suicide, which call for professional help, the message should be "I still like you as a person. Here are some ways I can restore my trust in you."

Try not to generalize a single mistake: "If I can't trust you to do this, then how can I trust you to do anything else?" With this type of attitude, how can a student ever regain your trust?

There is a tendency to judge the student before all the facts are known. At Roosevelt, nearly every teacher acts as an adviser-advocate for twenty-plus students. This means that when one of my advisees has a problem, I attend a conference with other teachers, students, and administrators involved and make certain that the student's point of view and feelings—I do not defend these—are heard and that the student is treated—and, it is hoped, feels treated—fairly. No matter what the outcome or the consequences, the student feels accepted and is open to continuing to work toward success.

There is a delicate balance between rehashing the past and using past happenings to demonstrate patterns. To keep reminding the student of all the failures and problems from past times in school only reinforces that the student is destined to keep acting this way in the future. Yet students often isolate their actions: "Well, I only did this once, or just in this class because of the teacher." In such cases, it's important to document other times the student has acted in similar ways to show a pattern to the student—or to others if necessary. The concern, however, is still how to improve, how to change, and where to go from here.

Maybe we can build trust in smaller chunks. Instead of saying "From now on you had better do all your homework" or "Never lie to me again," what if we say, "This week (or even the next two days) let's see you do all your homework, or let me know that I can trust whatever you say"? Then build little by little from there. A student can usually understand and manage the small chunk but has little concept of "never." The teacher can then appreciate the student's efforts and step-by-step accomplishments.

Shadowing

To learn what one student experiences in a day at school and to gain perspective into the way that student deals with school life, try a "shadow study program" with your staff. A teacher chooses a special student to shadow through the school day without the student's knowledge. Another way to assign teachers to students would be to put the names of students at different grade levels and with different levels of academic skills, cultural backgrounds, and behaviors can be put on slips of paper so participating teachers can draw names. It is better if the teacher can observe the student through an entire school day, but even a half-day would help. Observing also means being near that student when the student is in the halls, on break, or at lunch to observe what happens for that student at these times.

Each shadow teacher should jot down some observations about the student to share with the rest of the staff:

1. How did the student look—physical appearance and attitude—when the day began compared to when the day ended?

2. What type of social interactions did this student have with other students? With other adults? At lunch? In the halls?

3. How did this student behave during class? Did the student seem to understand the work? Follow directions? Cooperate in class? Work with other students? What were the classroom circumstances that either helped or hindered the student's success?

After the shadowing, another option is to take a short time to interview that student about what happened during the day and get the student's personal evaluation of the day and the school in general.

Finding the time and the money for substitute teachers to free the classroom teacher to participate in this study might be a problem. Perhaps the school could apply for a minigrant through the district or other organizations. Then, too, a group of teachers might combine to do something different that would release one or two teachers for a part of the day. If even six or ten members of the staff had this experience and shared what they learned with the rest of the staff, a lot of insight would be gained. As one teacher said, "We know some kids aren't happy in school. I want to know why and what we might do about it."

"Adopt" a Student

At one of his workshops, Stephen Glenn described how a group made up of an administrator, a teacher, and a counselor in inner-city Detroit worked together to supervise a small group of students from first through eighth grade. They kept close tabs on those students in school and out, even visiting the homes regularly. As a result, those students had a low absentee rate and few behavior problems and experienced success in school.

Well, not all schools can manage the time and cooperative effort to do this, but what happens if a teacher, or two teachers—as was suggested at our school—"adopt" a student? True, there are so many students in school who could be "adopted" that it might be difficult to choose, but focus on only one at-risk student.

You don't have to tell that person you're "adopting" him or her. Just keep more of a watch on that student. There are many small ways to help: a friendly, concerned reminder about work; an offer to explain something; a positive reinforcement for behavior, doing something well, or just being a nice person that day; stopping to talk, a smile, and "How are you?"; or maybe some little mystery gifts. Don't overlook "adopting" those quiet students who seldom talk or participate but never disrupt. Even the little, focused efforts just mentioned can do wonders for a student's self-image and satisfy the need to be valued.

Kid-Focused Staff Meetings

At least once a month, we should drop the ordinary business in our staff meetings and focus solely on kids. The counselor, vice-principal, nurse, and other teachers might discuss in an overview what they've observed happening with students in general, or with specific groups or individuals.

Some staff sessions might target specific students at risk. Those staff members who have had personal encounters and have background information on a particular student might share this with other staff members. All information, of course, would be understood to be confidential. The main purpose of the meeting would then be to determine how all staff people, including secretaries and custodians, can work together to improve this student's experience at school.

Give Encouragement

1. Give students responsibilities according to their capabilities that they're expected to follow through on.

2. Encourage them to participate in making significant decisions.

3. Ask students what they think about a matter and value what they say.

4. Express your appreciation for their contributions. Be specific: "Thanks for helping clean up the classroom," rather than "You're a good kid."

5. Accept their mistakes. Sometimes I purposely make a mistake on the board or on a handout, and the students catch it. Then I admit I made that mistake and thank them for finding it.

6. Expect students to do well and give them the chance to fulfill those expectations.

We know the way we treat a child forms a cause and effect relationship.

If a child lives with criticism he learns to condemn.
If a child lives with hostility he learns to fight.
If a child lives with ridicule he learns to be shy.
If a child lives with shame he learns to feel guilty.
If a child lives with tolerance he learns to be patient.
If a child lives with encouragement he learns confidence.
If a child lives with praise he learns to appreciate.
If a child lives with fairness he learns justice.
If a child lives with security he learns to have faith.
If a child lives with approval he learns to like himself.
If a child lives with acceptance and friendship he learns to find love in the world.

—Dorothy Law Nolte

REFERENCES

Asbury, Steve. 1993. "Dyslexia: The Hidden Disability." *South Eugene High Axe* (January 27): I-1–I-4. (Information from the Orton Dyslexia Society.)

Caine, R., and G. Caine. 1990. "Understanding a Brain-Based Approach to Learning and Teaching." *Educational Leadership* 48: 66-70.

Glenn, Stephen. 1990. "Developing Capable People" workshop. Portland, OR, March.

Golden, Nancy. 1990. "Students At-Risk" workshop. Roosevelt Middle School, Eugene, OR, January 3.

Kidder, Tracy. 1989. *Among School Children.* Boston: Houghton Mifflin.

Minton, Lynn. 1992. "Fresh Voices." *Parade* (May 31): 6.

Phelan, Patricia, Ann Locke Davidson, and Hanh Thanh Cao. 1992. "Speaking Up: Students' Perspectives on School." *Phi Delta Kappan* (May): 695-703.

Rottier, Jerry, Margie Stone, and Delaine Kinka. 1988. "Early Adolescence—A Time for Change: Implications for the Family." University of Wisconsin video.

Slemp, Jim. 1990. "From the Principal." *Roosevelt Middle School Community Newsletter* (March): 2.

Sousa, David. 1992. "How the Brain Learns." Presented to the National Staff Development Council, Washington, D.C. December 8.

"Turning Points: Preparing American Youth for the 21st Century." 1989. Carnegie Council on Adolescent Development workshop.

5

Let's Communicate

A child is a person who is going to carry out what you have started. . . . He will assume control of your cities, states and nations, he is going to move in and take over your churches, schools, universities and corporations. . . . The face of humanity is in his hands.
—Abraham Lincoln

HOW DO YOU COMMUNICATE WITH STUDENTS?

In one of the personal communication classes I taught, one girl told the class, "When someone yells at me, all I want to do is run away. I don't hear anything that person's saying. I shut my ears and want to get out of there!" If the student can't run away physically from a yelling, angry teacher in a classroom, then certainly the student can—and does—run away mentally and emotionally, just for self-preservation.

Anger, threats, humiliating put-downs, and sarcasm, have little, if any, place in the classroom. These actions do not encourage communication, participation, understanding, or positive learning. They do create resentment, opportunities to gain revenge, and negative feelings about teachers and learning.

Michael Grinder, a noted educator, mentioned in one of his workshops on learning styles that studies show that giving directions in the negative produces negative results. When you say, "Don't run in the hall" or "Don't talk," most people do not hear the negative, just the command itself. So they run in the hall or talk, and often legitimately don't know why the teacher responds in such a negative way. It's far more effective to say, "Please walk," "Please slow down," or "Please be quiet now."

Choose one teaching day—or better yet a week of classes—to keep track of the number of negative comments you make to students. Jot down the number of negative comments at the end of each period or time block and, if you can remember, why you made them—what were the situations—and to whom? If

it's later in the term, do you find that those comments are consistently directed at a few students who may not be working or cooperating well?

I could never locate the exact source, but several years ago, a staff member mentioned that he had read, I believe in *Scientific American*, that there are over seventy different ways a person can receive a message. This holds immense implications for teachers communicating with students, and vice versa. When a teacher says, "I told you the test would cover . . . ," this does not necessarily mean that each student in the class heard what the teacher said, received the same message, and interpreted it in the same way. Each student has a different learning style. So you have to communicate that message on the board, possibly on paper, and orally, and to repeat the message several times. Even though a teacher may have given directions, the student may not have understood the message, and this may not be the student's fault.

In teaching a class, give students time to digest and understand the material and concepts. Don't lecture on and on for a forty-minute period. Ask students questions about the general topic, questions about the specific material, not just to test whether they were listening, but to understand how they feel about what you said and how it applies to their lives. If you're discussing the arrival of slavery in America, ask how it affected African Americans then and how it still affects them today.

If members in the class don't respond, or only a few do, direct your questions to individual students in an informal, inviting way. Form small groups and ask those in the group to respond to one or two point-of-view questions you give them. Also, solicit from the group questions they have about slavery, this time period, and what happened. Then have a spokesperson from each group report back to the entire class.

Open the door for any student to offer an opinion safely. Establish guidelines in your class specifying that no one is allowed to mock, laugh, or ridicule someone else's opinion. You yourself would not do these things. Students should also be allowed to state their views without those views being judged right or wrong. Allow students to question the validity of the statements, materials, and concepts you present.

Open questioning is a vital part of learning and understanding. Students respect calm, reasoned, sincere responses from you both as a person and as a teacher. You should do the same, allowing the student to disagree with your conclusions and encouraging the student to state reasons for that disagreement. It's a tribute to you as a teacher and an exhilarating feeling for the student when the student feels comfortable enough in class to stand up and say, "I don't agree with you for this and that reason," knowing that you will sincerely listen to what the student says.

We often talk about students who "fall through the cracks." There have been too many times when it's been midterm before I've realized a student doesn't understand the material, hasn't been learning, has some personal problem I've not been informed about, or has been "faking me out." Often, these are the quiet students who sit in corners, maybe smile, rarely answer questions, but seem nice and cooperative. In many cases, these students want and need help but don't know how to ask for it and feel embarrassed. It's important for you to focus on them in quiet, unobtrusive ways to see if they need help.

> The literal translation of the Latin term meaning *to educate* is *to draw forth from within.*

Some teachers find it useful to take the "pulse of the class." They suspend the lesson for a moment and ask the class, or ask individual students: "On a scale of one to five, five being the greatest, how are you feeling about what we're studying?" The students hold up fingers to show their feelings. If a number of students give low scores, it's important to stop and ask them why they feel that way—for they may be the honest ones. A low score means that something is interfering with learning. There is little point in continuing the lesson unless you have some sense of how to improve the way you're communicating and the lesson.

With the same objective, you might ask students—in an encouraging, nonjudgmental way—to tell you two or three new things or ideas they've just learned in class. You could also do this by having them quickly jot down three things they learned. It's fine if not all the students write down the same three items. If you're feeling confident and brave, ask the students to write a personal evaluation of the day's lesson: What did they learn? What does it mean to them? How well was the lesson taught?

ON A ONE-TO-ONE BASIS

When a student comes to you with a question, a request for help, or a personal problem, find the time to listen and give that help. However, you need to determine the best time to meet with that person. You might suggest the student come the next day before class, or stay for a few minutes after class if that's possible and if you feel the student's concern can be addressed briefly.

However, if it's obvious that you do need to take some time with the student, suggest a more appropriate block of time and make certain you keep the appointment. Imagine a young person who feels in a personal crisis, works up to the point of trying to come to you to deal with it at a specified time, and then you don't show, are late, cut it short, or have numerous interruptions.

When the student comes to you or when you have a conference with a student and others, you might consider doing the following:

1. Arrange chairs or desks so that you are sitting next to, not opposite or at a higher level than, the student. (When I talk with students during class, I often kneel next to desks so that my eye level is equal to theirs. I find

this helps alleviate any feelings of intimidation or domination (by adult authority) students might experience.

2. If you have a specific concern, simply state the reason you are meeting. Then ask if the student understands or has any questions. If the student has asked to meet with you, allow the student to state the reason for the meeting and the concern without interruptions or "corrections."

3. When the student or someone else is speaking, listen with your whole body. Look at the person who is talking. Lean forward to show your attention. Don't interrupt with questions or comments.

4. Allow students to express their feelings about the situation however they choose. If students "hate" the class or feel like a failure, it doesn't help to tell the students that they don't really hate the class or that they're not failures. Just acknowledge those feelings. For the students, those feelings and perceptions are real. Even if you feel the students are way off target, your feelings don't matter at this point. If the students' ideas seem odd, not in accord with your own, accept their perceptions and listen anyway. You must deal with the students' feelings and perceptions. Remember how it was when you were a student and how teachers listened—or didn't listen—to your concerns and feelings.

5. Comments such as "I hate this class" or "I can't do the work" are too emotional and abstract to deal with in any practical way. Help the student clarify and focus the concern. "What exactly do you hate about this class? You can say whatever you want. It's okay." Or "I can see you feel you can't do the work, but, specifically, what confuses you about the work we do in this class? Try to list some things for me." With concrete detail, you have more to discuss and more chance of helping solve the problem. (The multitude and variety of talk shows on both radio and television demonstrates how many people—mainly adults, in this case—are overwhelmed by the problems of just living in our contemporary world. Imagine how children, who are largely ignored and powerless in our society, feel. Listen to or watch some of these shows. Notice how the host interacts with the caller or guests and draws from them the concrete details needed to discuss the situation. Notice also what you don't like about the way many of these hosts treat their guests: how they interrupt, don't listen at times, come across as too harsh, or are impatient or objectionable.)

6. When the student has finished stating the concern, take a moment to restate what was said to make certain you understand. "You hate math because you cannot do the computations quickly enough on tests, or in your head. Is that what you mean?"

You might ask—even assist—the student in describing his or her feelings about a situation and then, filtering out the emotions, try to describe the actual incident objectively. After that, ask the student how the other party (even if that party is you) might have seen the situation and felt about what happened.

7. Before you jump in with suggestions, invest the student with some sense of power. You might ask, "What have you done to try to solve this problem? What happened when you tried this? Why do you think it didn't work for you?" (When you were a youth, how often were you empowered by adults to resolve your own conflicts? Given the chance, how did you feel when you discovered you could resolve your own problems and keep them from lingering and festering?)

Following this, you might ask the student to suggest other ways to solve this problem and how to do it effectively, considering and projecting the outcomes of various actions. "If you hit the kid because you're angry, what will be the result?" "If you ask this person, 'Can we sit down somewhere by ourselves and talk about what's been happening?' then what may be the results?"

Next, you might ask, "Would you like me to make some suggestions that might help?" If the student says no, that's fine. Don't be offended. You asked, and the student is giving an honest response. Maybe the student just isn't ready to accept your help or feels intimidated by you. Maybe just having the chance to talk with you and express feelings was enough.

If the answer is yes, offer two or three suggestions. "You might try …." You don't want to overwhelm the student with all sorts of possibilities, and too many suggestions could be humiliating and counterproductive. With each suggestion, brainstorm with the student on ways to put that idea into action. (It's aggravating for someone to say, "Oh, it's easy! Just do this.")

8. Leave the door open for the student to return to you for more discussion or help. Set up a check time in a few days or a week, not more, to see if things have improved for the student.

If things have improved, great! Work with the student to write a list of exactly what's improved—even the small steps: "I turned in one more assignment this week than last." Then write down the next goals to achieve. In this way, the student and you can see and record the progress made.

If things haven't improved, work with the student to make a list of exactly what has not improved, how the student tried to improve, and why those efforts didn't work. There may be more improvement evident than either you or the student may think.

Keep any of these lists in a student file, or make copies for yourself and give the student the originals. These will be invaluable references as time passes. Parents might want to see the lists, too.

9. If the student rejects all help and won't make any efforts to improve, perhaps the student will discuss with you why no effort was made. If the student

won't, try a different type of list. Welcome the student to join you in listing what may happen if the student doesn't succeed, socially or academically at school, or can't resolve the problem. "If you don't pass this particular class, what do you think will be the consequences?" If there's no response, then state the consequences: "Then you won't be able to . . . , or you will have to take . . ." "If you continue to steal or harass others or cause behavior problems in class, then . . ."

You may make this list in terms of immediate consequences and also long-term projections, building these in a step-by-step process so the student can see the connection. "If you don't complete school, you won't have a high school diploma. Without a diploma today, what work will you do? How will you buy your car and keep it? Buy food? Find a place to live?"

Keep a copy of this list in a file. Make certain you give the student a copy, too. Send a third copy home to the parents with the suggestion that they discuss this with their child. And leave your door open for the student to come back to you.

These points are difficult to accept but are worth remembering:

1. You cannot control each student in your room. You cannot control students' behaviors, their desires to learn, or their successes in learning. All you can do is control yourself—model with your own behavior, desire to learn, and demonstrated willingness to help students learn.

2. It's futile to try to defend yourself and your value judgments through logical arguments with students, especially if either of you is angry.

3. The trick is to bring the students into the process, to offer choices within established boundaries rather than saying, "Yes, you can" or "No, you can't." It's better to say, "You have the choice of doing this or this."

4. Take a moment to think of what you were like as a teenager. Certainly you responded best when there was understanding, empathy, and gentle humor from another.

People find what they're looking for. If you're looking for conspiracies, you'll find conspiracies. If you're looking for examples of man's good works, you'll find that, too. It's all a matter of setting your mental channel.
—Roger von Oech
A Kick in the Seat of the Pants

POSITIVE DISCIPLINE

Again and again, the national studies on education in the United States call for more discipline in the schools. The public feels that students need stricter discipline and that teachers must exert more control over student behavior in the school and in the classroom. The same horror stories of student misbehavior are recounted as the standard condition in our schools.

We teachers often don't recognize that most students function well, cooperate, attend classes, are responsible, and don't cause problems. Instead, we dwell on the 3 or 5 percent of those students who do cause difficulties, and we often make rules to restrict and punish everyone, in advance, for those 3 percent.

In a Roosevelt parent newsletter, our principal noted:

- 98% of our students have *not* been suspended out of school.

- 98% of our students were *not* disciplined for fighting.

- 99% of our students have *not* been involved in vandalism.

- 96% of our students arrive on time for classes each day.

If so many students function so well at school, then why do we react the way we do? Why do we impose so many rules and consequences that often cause more problems and more feelings of injustice?

No eating in the hallway.

Walk on the right-hand side only.

Students who are late to class, no matter what the excuse, will be locked out of the classroom. (Would we adults stand for such treatment?)

Then we lie in wait to pounce on transgressors, to inflict punishments—often way out of proportion to the "crime."

Do you—as I do—remember how it felt to be treated this way, seeing the teachers and administrators as the enemy, especially in the hallways? I remember the energy we invested in fooling the teachers, in purposely bugging them. I don't want my students to see me this way. It serves no purpose in terms of positive communication or positive learning. I enjoy having students come to me, smiling, to say hello, tell me about something exciting or funny that happened to them, express concerns, ask questions. I enjoy them knowing that I'm there for them.

Perhaps instead of making strictness the goal, educators should focus on developing true discipline in students, stressing individual self-control and personal responsibility to self and to others. For the past twenty-five years, teachers have tried such an approach at Roosevelt Middle School. They expect students to be responsible and to behave well. And, in general, the students do.

But Roosevelt teachers have not left students completely to their own devices. A support system of teacher-advisers to guide students has been established so that a teacher can help students when they have problems and act as an advocate for a student to help explain, not defend, the student's view. Each teacher at Roosevelt acts as an adviser for approximately twenty-two sixth-, seventh-, and eighth-grade students who belong to what we call a "house." There are currently forty such houses at Roosevelt—even the principal and counselor each have a house—a marvelous way to keep them in touch with everyday school happenings and the concerns of students.

Teachers and administrators also distinguish between minor and major problems. For such minor problems as tardiness, unexcused absences, minor disruptive behavior, not doing homework, being unprepared for class, or talking in class, a teacher either sends a note to the involved student's adviser, or sends the student to the adviser to discuss the problem.

If necessary, the adviser and the student meet with the teacher to discuss the matter in a calm, rational atmosphere. At such a meeting, the student has the opportunity to present a personal point of view of the situation to both the teacher and the adviser and to find out why the teacher reacted in a particular way. It may seem obvious why the student was sent out of class, but very often it's not so obvious to the student: "I just asked my friend for a pencil, and the teacher told me to get out!" It may have been the tenth time the student spoke out in class that period, but the student tends to see only isolated incidents, not the complete picture.

> When I see the '10 most wanted list' . . . I always have this thought: If we'd made them feel wanted earlier, they wouldn't be wanted now.
> —Eddie Cantor

This communication process is central to helping students learn self-control and be responsible for their own behavior and fosters in them the feeling that they are a valuable part of the school process. If they don't understand what they've done and why it's a problem, how can they change?

There have also been those times when the student shouldn't have been disciplined in a particular way and the teacher was way out of line. This meeting should help illustrate to the teacher how the situation could have been handled differently and that the student may have a legitimate concern or right to feel mistreated.

At Roosevelt, most teachers do not simply demand obedience and then expect students to change their attitudes immediately. Minor problems are worked out through mutual understanding. Perhaps the teacher also needs to make some changes in attitude and behavior.

Of course, there are occasional major problems, caused by a very small percentage of the total student population. For example, a student may get into a fight, bring a weapon to school, be insubordinate or verbally abusive, vandalize, steal, not cooperate with a substitute teacher, or harass others. Dealing with such situations is an administrative matter. Usually the student's adviser is called on to act as an advocate (one who states but not necessarily supports the student's position) for the student. In this way, the lines of communication remain open. Afterward the student can talk freely with the adviser or administrator about the problem. The goal is to prevent confrontations that pit the school against the student.

Minor offenses that are repeated often and cannot be resolved with a note home or a phone call to the parent become administrative matters, too.

Using this system frees administrators to deal with the 2 percent or 5 percent of the students who cause most of the serious problems in school. Focusing attention on these problem students allows the school to do without many rigid rules.

The absence of numerous rules has a number of benefits for both students and staff members. For example, teachers do not have assigned lunchroom duty. Even in an overcrowded school with 800 middle-schoolers, problems in the lunchroom are few. The counselor or an administrator usually roams the lunchroom. Most of the time they walk around, stopping to chat with the students, and they keep the atmosphere relaxed. Sometimes teachers voluntarily eat in the lunchroom just to talk with their students.

Do you remember how important lunch was to you during the school day? Often, it was the only time to be with friends. Students are allowed to eat lunch in the halls. This is an important socializing time for most students. In our rigid, rushed school day with its limited passing times, students have little time to relax and be with their peers socially, an important part of growing up and living in society.

In many other countries' schools, students have fifteen to twenty minutes or more between classes. They can relax, use the restroom, get something to eat or drink, visit with friends, become mentally renewed and prepared for a different curriculum. (Where in our society, besides the public schools, do we have this artificial system of a series of seven or eight 40- or 50-minute periods with 4-minute passing times in which students have to mentally keep jumping from one subject to another?)

Eating in the halls sometimes creates problems with litter, but seldom does it lead to any other problems. Usually, a morning consciousness-raising announcement by the principal about the litter and a request for help resolves the problem. At times, the hall is closed to eating for several days as a consequence. It is then reopened with good results.

Teachers do not have hall duty at Roosevelt—not even during the ten-minute morning break. They mill around, talk, and joke in the halls. Teachers and administrators move freely about the halls, talking with each other and with students, carrying on whatever business they have. Most often, a simple "Let's stop that before someone gets hurt" works just fine. Between classes, at lunchtime, and during the morning break, there is no sense of having to closely supervise students. In general, the atmosphere among students, teachers, and administrators is open and positive.

These positive feelings have also translated into several all-school activities. For example, during Beautification Day, members of houses went out and picked up litter; cleaned walls and lockers; planted trees, flowers, and bushes; and painted basketball courts and four-square lines on the playground. An art class designed and directed the creation of colorful murals in the hallways. Such activities could be extended to a community service project in an elementary school, a nursing home, or a pre-school. What a great way to foster community involvement, respect for teens, and teens' sense of self-worth!

After the Rodney King trial, some university students and other adults decided to stage a demonstration in front of Roosevelt during lunch. This, of course, attracted a good number of students, especially because many students have parent-approved passes to cross the street to eat lunch. When the bell rang for class, despite the pleas and harangues from the demonstrators, most of the students went back into the building. Then, some of the demonstrators forced their way into the building, ran through the halls, and banged on doors. They shouted at students to come out and join them, called students in the rooms a variety of names, and told them to break windows. The amazing and wonderful part is that the Roosevelt students didn't. They didn't break windows, didn't turn on their teachers, didn't try to leave the rooms. As a result, we survived this potentially dangerous time without any students or staff suffering injuries, without any violent police confrontations, and without any damage to school property!

After this, a group of Roosevelt students asked the administration if they could organize a half-day devoted to a series of workshops on racial and cultural prejudice. These students planned the day themselves and went out into the community to personally contact people to lead the workshop sessions. They created a meaningful school experience in which students attended some of over seventy workshops. This is learning!

A school administration with a long tradition of rigid rules and strictly enforced obedience would have a difficult time changing its policies to resemble those at Roosevelt. However, such a change, managed in a positive way and generated by the staff itself and the administration, can reduce stress in the classroom and allow teachers to pay more attention to teaching than to enforcing rules. Such a change can also bring about greater personal growth on the part of students and a warmer, more personal, and more productive relationship among students, teachers, administrators, and parents.

6

Teaching!

Life is either an exciting adventure or it is nothing at all!
—Helen Keller

WHAT WE KNOW

Teaching happens, not through a knowledge base alone, but rather through a combination of the head, the hands, and the heart. We must understand, experience, and feel to teach effectively.

As teachers, to make learning an exciting and successful adventure for our students, we need to first recognize, consider, and incorporate some of the things we know about learning and teaching into our work with students. Students become turned on to school when learning involves and focuses on allowing them to examine their own lives and express their feelings sincerely and openly, knowing their perspectives will be valued.

Learning is shaped by the student's prior knowledge, happens a great deal through social interaction, has close ties to particular people and situations, and involves the use of numerous approaches and techniques. We learn from one another, from sharing and working together, not from books alone.

When empowered, people learn. Empowerment for the student happens when there is dialogue between the teacher and the student and between the student and other students. It also happens when there is interaction between more knowledgeable and experienced people and less knowledgeable and experienced people. Empowerment for the student happens when there is collaboration and cooperation among learners; firmness and positive discipline with dignity and respect; and an acknowledgment of the value of the person and that person's ideas, values, feelings, and effort.

Students—or for that matter, people—do not trust others who talk *at* them, not with them; who do things to or for them; or who treat any person as a stereotype of a group rather than as an individual.

We know that all students will have to prepare for an increasingly multicultural world with global implications. This means students and teachers must be able to change mind-sets, commitments, and view ideas and events through multiple perspectives.

We know that people from various cultures come to school with different work attitudes, concepts of time and space, languages, role expectations and models, group values and individual allegiances, rituals and superstitions, concepts of class and status, and ethical values. By the year 2000, one of every three schoolchildren will be from a minority people. At present, in twenty-five of our twenty-six largest urban school districts, minority students outnumber white students.

Although our society keeps undergoing dramatic and rapid technological and social transformation, our schools have not changed essentially for the past 150 years. Today, our high schools are not working for a majority of the kids because our schools and education system are driven by political values, not educational values.

Students must feel that courses and content are directly relevant to the true business of life—to survival outside the artificiality of the traditional school setting. Students work much more successfully and enjoy learning if they like what they are doing and feel supported and encouraged to explore. They work much less successfully and will resent learning if they are made to feel afraid to express themselves or are afraid of failure. Failures (not chronic failure), mistakes or errors in judgment, are part of the learning process and should be approached as such. The focus must be on the problem and not the person, what was learned from the failure or mistake, and how this experience can be used in positive ways.

We know that children need exercise to feel good, to be able to concentrate, and to be in a physically and emotionally healthy state to learn. Sitting at desks for long periods of time severely hinders the ability and enjoyment of learning for most children. Health and fitness improve academic performance and reduce behavior problems.

Teachers need to incorporate a wide array of approaches to meet different student needs, interests, and varied intelligences. When a teacher works with students, that teacher must do so in writing, visually, orally, and kinesthetically. As Will Rogers noted: "If the only tool in your toolbox is a hammer, then everything is a nail." In all aspects of their work with students, teachers must be flexible.

We know that young people need *time* to think and play and dream. Many of our great scientists, explorers, and artists had the perceptions and the curiosity of a child. The arts and applied arts—music, drama, drawing and painting, metalwork, woodcraft, auto repair, sewing—provide the main opportunity for creativity and self-discipline in school. They are vital outlets and often provide learning success for the more than eighty percent of our students who do not lend themselves to the linear-logical approach to learning, upon which most schools insist. For many at-risk, abused students, the arts and applied arts provide a concrete sense of recognition, self-worth, and accomplishment seldom found anywhere else in the school curriculum.

> The artist is not a different
> kind of person,
> but every person is a different
> kind of artist.
> —Eric Gill, Philosopher

In New York City, the nation's center for the arts, two-thirds of the city's public elementary schools have no art or music teachers. Yet in Germany and Japan, schoolchildren are required to study the arts every year of schooling, and the schools devote much more classroom time to the arts than do U.S. schools. "Forty-one percent of the human race cannot learn on a forty-minute bell schedule" (Glenn 1991).

A study (Barker, et al. 1981) on personal communication noted that of the people surveyed, 53 percent listened as part of their communication, 17 percent read, 16 percent talked, and 9 percent wrote. In school we spend the greatest amount of time teaching writing, the communication skill used least often in the outside world. We spend the least amount of time—if we do so at all—teaching listening, the communication skill most used and most critical in the outside world. Especially in the world of work (Steil 1978).

Finally, we know that January through March are the worst months to educate because this is a period of little sunlight, warmth, and growth. In nature, this is a period of hibernation. We *are* part of nature (Glenn 1991).

SKILLS FOR THE TWENTY-FIRST CENTURY

New technology allows students to work individually and cooperatively, mastering process and learning skills needed for the next century. According to Amy Klaulke, educator, we do not know what seven of ten jobs will be like in the twenty-first century; it is forecast that on average, each person will change jobs six or seven times. She believes we will need the ability to think and reason abstractly; understand and communicate complex ideas; work cooperatively with others; analyze and use resources; and solve complex problems. Jamieson McKenzie (1987) pointed out that to prepare our students with these skills for the twenty-first century, we must teach

- data analysis,

- risk-taking as opposed to fear of failure,

- originality,

- working in groups to share talents and solve problems,

- thinking skills,
- the arts,
- how to best and effectively use leisure time,
- physical fitness and health, and
- interdependence.

Doyle and Pimentel (1993, 43), summarize what's in and what's out for the 1990s:

OUT	IN
Innate Ability	Effort
Rote Learning	Mastery
Autocratic Teachers	Autonomous Students
Seat Time in Class	Accomplishment
Student as Learner	Student as Worker
Teacher as Lecturer	Teacher as Manager
Administrator as Master	Administrator as Servant
Periods, semesters, years	Flexible Schedules
Diploma = Seat Time	Diploma = Mastery
Age	Accomplishment
Community as Taxpayer	Parent as Shareholder
Teacher as Blue Collar Worker	Teacher as Professional
True and False Tests	Authentic Assessment
Uniform Salary Schedule	Pay for Scarcity and Performance
Education as the School's Business	Education as Everyone's Business
School = Building	School = Learning

TEACHING CREATIVITY AND THINKING SKILLS

As Howard Gardner noted in his book *Frames of Mind* (1983), people have different intelligences—seven different ones—and each person uses a particular intelligence as the primary, not the only, way to understand and learn. These seven intelligences are linear, logical, musical, spatial, kinesthetic, interpersonal, and intrapersonal.

In school, we focus mainly on the linear and logical approach to learning. Stephen Glenn stated that 85 percent of students do not tend toward linear, logical learning. As a result, 80 percent of American children lose their desire to risk and their natural creativity when they enter this type of narrow-approach, punishing learning situation in our schools.

> What kind of a world will we have if students can't think? Today, they can't think!
>
> —Nancy Ellis
> nationally-known educator

Many students who have demonstrated great intelligence in various symbol systems and alternative approaches to learning just do not have the specific intelligence that is required to learn in many of our schools. That such specific intelligence is required in order to be successful is evidence of some teachers' and schools' rigidity and narrow expectations. Flexibility and adaptability are qualities school educators expect in students but sometimes do not pay sufficient attention to in their own professional development. Students learn by example.

Dr. Thomas Armstrong pointed out that different cultures emphasize different types of intelligences. In Hungary, for example, everyone is expected to be musically literate. A Hungarian child who is not musically literate would, according to American educational thought, be labeled low-skilled. When we label a child as disabled, or low-skilled, Dr. Armstrong wondered what has happened to teachers' awareness and understanding of the student's other six intelligences? "We each have gifts never developed because they were not honored by schools" (1992).

From these observations, we understand that creativity isn't only a matter of genetics but that all children possess creativity with one or more of these seven intelligences. Teachers have the responsibility to help students discover and to nurture the students creative bents. Such support encourages students to risk; students gain the self-confidence to reach out and explore other ways of learning and other areas of knowledge and skills.

Perhaps the prime ingredient in encouraging creativity, the development of thinking skills, and the utilization of a person's predominant type of intelligence is problem solving. The student defines the problem and uses the intelligence or the approach that the student, not the teacher, feels will best solve the problem. If that approach doesn't work, then the student, possibly with the teacher's guidance, reexamines the outcomes and the original problem and determines another approach to solving it. "We can teach for creativity at any level, in any field. And if we want to improve our children and our nation, this is exactly what we need to do" (Sternberg and Lubart 1991, 608-14).

Dr. Edward deBono (1989), author and educator, emphasized that thinking is a skill and that, like any skill, it can be developed and strengthened. If we can learn to free ourselves of rigid methodology, free ourselves to think, especially with the right brain, we can create innumerable approaches and solutions to problems. We should encourage students to offer all possible suggestions on how to make better use of ideas or solve the problem.

Our Western competitive approach has stressed that we must destroy the current model, pointing out the flaws, in order to supplant it with a new and supposedly better one. Eastern thought, however, focuses on the strengths or positive elements in the present model, on retaining these and searching together for ways to build and improve on them. Precious energy and emotion is not wasted on destroying but is instead utilized to build.

Dr. deBono has developed his "six hats" approach to help people think and speak in different ways when problem-solving. Each "hat" has a narrow and specific focus, and people can function in that mode only when wearing that hat:

- The first hat is for seeking data and information that might be needed.

- The second hat allows people to freely express their *emotions and feelings* about the topic or problem. The person does not and should not have to explain or justify these feelings, just voice them.

- The third hat allows people to state the *reasons* something cannot be done or the weaknesses in carrying out the task in a certain way.

- The fourth hat is for focusing on the *reasons* something *can* be done: benefits, opportunities that will occur.

- The fifth hat is the *creative* hat and is used to generate brainstorming and risk-taking, possibilities, and "what-ifs." In this stage, shifting paradigms should be encouraged (negative feelings or reasons may not be expressed here).

- The sixth and last hat is worn when one wants to look at how the group is thinking and how the process is working and is also the hat for planning and defining next steps to take.

These hats all have the same value; they allow thinking and exploration to happen without the personal investment that dominates, dictates, and destroys the educational progress and creative thinking.

DeBono noted that creative thinking requires time to think each day, a focus on targets to choose and think about, reasons to think about a target, and techniques on how to think. When do we allow and teach our students to do this?

Sternberg and Lubart (1991) stated that creative people more frequently pose questions to explore rather than concern themselves with solutions. The questions intrigue and stimulate thinking.

So what would happen if we applied all of the foregoing to changing class periods so they work more effectively and flexibly, to improving the school environment, to exploring ways young people can be involved in the community, and to helping young people stay off drugs?

> People who are resting on their laurels are wearing them on the wrong end.
> —Malcolm Kushner, Philosopher

Ask each person in class to do one thing differently during the next twenty-four hours. Students can tell the class the next day what they did, how it made them feel, the results, and if they would do it that way again and why.

Ask students to choose any two common nouns from the dictionary. How can they combine those two words to make a new product or service? Suggest brainstorming and making lists of uses of the noun, parts of the word, and associations for each word. Once they have a new product or service, who would use it and how? How would they market it?

Another shifting-paradigm, creative approach might focus on reversal. Brainstorm some ways that "I can be a worse teacher or worse student or worse child or worse driver." What are five rules you can break today? This can be a lot of fun!

In the same manner, what point of view in a given situation would be your dog, a chair you sit on, a ball you hit with a bat, the cliffs overlooking the ocean, or an audiocassette have?

How about a preventative approach! What could we do to prevent hurricanes? How could we stop plane crashes? What would make the cafeteria food good to eat? How could we teach dogs and cats to get along with each other?

Ask students to respond to "what-if" questions that produce strange, creative thoughts. Some examples might be: What if a genie existed in New York City? What if horses were doctors? What if the Mafia was exiled to Mars?

You could also ask students to make up metaphors and explain them:

Dealing with your parents is like _____.

Taking a final exam is like _____.

Trying to get money is like _____.

Eating a hot fudge sundae is like _____.

Stephen Glenn mentioned that in one elementary school production of *Cinderella*, one boy decided to play a barking pig. Now this class's version of *Cinderella* has a barking pig in it! Why not? (In other versions of the story—not the familiar American one—Cinderella is a clever girl who tries to escape and save herself; she doesn't just sit and accept her situation. In these versions, Cinderella *thinks creatively*.)

As psychologist James Hillman observed, using imagination and creativity helps students not only to think but also to openly express emotions that otherwise, if repressed, might get out of control. "My practice shows me rather that the more attuned and experienced the imaginative side of personality the less threatening the irrational, the less necessity for repression, and therefore the less actual pathology acted out in literal, daily events " (1979).

WHAT DO WE TEACH AND HOW?

We know that essential skills—thinking, communication, cooperative learning, listening, reading, writing, speaking, math, and research—can be incorporated into any subject area. For years, I've taught a sports history class that incorporates all of these skills. We compute and track various sports statistics, invent new sports products, imitate sports routines or happenings, read about sports or famous sports figures, and discuss current sports issues. One time we reenacted the trial of Shoeless Joe Jackson. We also learn to play games from other cultures, create jokes and puns about sports, and research in groups a particular sport and present that information to the class in oral and written forms.

Before our people went to school, we worked together hunting a seal or skinning a caribou.
In school we learned that to cooperate is to cheat.
Before the schools came, we were a spiritual people. We believed that animals, plants, and people were all living beings. We had a reverence for life. Indeed the essence of our life was spiritual.
Now everything is cognitive.
Our children used to dance
                and celebrate
                    and be filled with joy.
Now they must sit still in their seats, where they face a never-ending parade of abstract learning and symbols.
                    —A Native American elder from a small Alaskan tribe

---

We know that to teach knowledge for the sake of knowledge alone is not effective because students do not retain information unless they can see the connections: Why is this knowledge important and how will it be useful? How, specifically, will the information help the student survive in the world? As I once heard Howard Gardner say, it's not how smart you are—but how are you smart? that's most important.

If listening is 53 percent of our communication, then it seems an important skill for students to learn. Larry Littlebird (1991), noted Native American storyteller and author, points out the difference between hearing and listening: We all use our ears to hear sounds that come from many different directions, but the act of listening—understanding and interpreting—is an act we must *learn* to do. Before, through mainly story, we would learn this skill as a member of a tribe or community of extended family. Today, seldom is there an immediate, much less an extended, family; school becomes the community where students can learn this vital skill.

Eighty-nine percent of people in their twenties who lose their jobs lose them not due to a lack of academic skills but rather because they don't know how to listen, follow directions, and get along with others on the job (Glenn 1990). "If learning to listen was as simple as hearing then what a different world we would live in. . . . What I do know is that in an oral culture, learning to listen is the beginning of all learning" (Littlebird 1991, 3).

> When we tell students to "learn" something,
> what do we expect them to do?
> —Bill Kentta, Curriculum Specialist

We certainly want students to learn to express themselves openly, clearly, informally, and in an interesting way. The traditional speech class does not help the majority of students accomplish this. In fact, it does the opposite in most instances, intimidating the vast majority, who will never get up in front of a group to make a formal speech. (Several years ago, a survey on people's greatest fears listed death as the third greatest fear and public speaking as the number one fear.)

One of the most effective ways to help students successfully learn these skills and enjoy speaking is to teach them storytelling. Children are natural storytellers and love to share their stories, both fiction and nonfiction. Incorporating theater games, improvisational and reader's theatre, and little skits or plays in low-key, nonthreatening ways helps open up even some of the shyest students to sharing orally. You can do any and all these activities in any type of class.

Students need knowledge and information to accomplish tasks. However, information today is overwhelming, doubling every twelve months! No one can be an "all-knowing expert" anymore, though certain people can have expertise in a field. Now, students must learn how to find information, select information they need for a particular project or purpose, organize and present that information in a variety of ways, and evaluate what they have done.

Cooperative learning allows students to pool their various learning strengths and individual skills, to learn from each other, to share (something we expect them to do but perhaps have not taught them how to do), and to accomplish individual and group tasks. With the cooperative approach, students can develop their social and communication skills in constructive ways, can exercise some control over what they would like to accomplish, and can choose projects that are meaningful to them.

Schools must have more flexible and different time schedules. Glenn noted that forty-one percent of the human race cannot learn on a forty-minute class schedule. Students can't learn and understand the material in seven or eight unrelated classes a day with four-minute passing times. Where else in our society do we learn like this? Even college students don't endure this type of scheduling. In most schools in other parts of the world, students do not suffer such a rushed, fragmented learning experience. Some schools have found that altering schedules to incorporate block periods, increasing time between classes, and alternate-day classes do a great deal to reduce stress for both students and teachers. We don't want courses to be forgotten but rather used and applied, or what's the point of education?

We know that we don't teach history or English or science: We teach kids! William Glasser said, "We should never forget that people, not curriculum, are the desired outcome of schooling. What we want to develop are students who have the skills to become active contributors to society, who are enthusiastic about what they have learned, and who are aware of how learning can be of use to them in the future" (1992, 694).

If you happen to teach in an elective program like Roosevelt's, then you can create any class—as long as it defines agreed-upon educational objectives and outcomes for students and fulfills program needs. What classes students choose indicates interest. These interests change: A class popular ten years ago may not be popular today. (I love sports—playing and watching—but I remember how I hated and dreaded the boring, humiliating PE classes in junior high and high school. If I had had a choice of offerings—bowling, tennis, soccer, physical fitness—and teachers, that would have made a great difference!) Middle school classes can be offered on Shakespeare, net games, "being yourself," small engine repair, computer graphics, international foods, building sets for plays, Hitler and the holocaust. Teachers might brainstorm with the students to come up with class possibilities and also to find out how students would like to learn in these classes.

As an alternative approach, conduct a school or grade survey. For language arts classes, you could list areas: literature, writing, other language arts classes. Under each area, list class ideas teachers and other students have suggested: Native American literature, mysteries, science fiction, short stories, movies and writing, ghost story writing, radio drama, storytelling. At the end of the survey, ask for other ideas, perhaps providing suggestions for topic areas, such as space, politics, humor, television, historical events, bookmaking, Jack London, or magazines.

After students have registered for a class on a certain topic, the teacher and students could brainstorm on what specific areas they would like to study within that topic, how they will approach it, what the students and teacher each will be responsible for, and how each will be evaluated.

See what happens, and then be open to ways to develop a class with that particular focus. Sometimes you have to scramble for materials, but with the help of librarians, computers, ERIC searches, the Internet, magazine articles, guest speakers, community people with expertise, videos, and, above all, creativity, a lot of resources are available. The orchestra teacher and I teamed up to teach a full-year class in the history of musical theater. We certainly did scramble for materials, but the students also did a lot of original research on projects. They created their own dramatic presentations, wrote original songs and music, played music on their instruments, and brought in guests, materials, and ideas we hadn't even known existed. The students' talents and resourcefulness amazed us! They wanted the course to work.

When we teach any subject, we must take the time to walk the student through the process. It's interesting, as Dr. Robert Marzano (1992) mentioned, that in teaching math in an American school, we pressure the students to do 100 problems in thirty minutes. In the Japanese schools, the teacher may walk the students through just two problems in thirty minutes to make certain each student understands.

Learn to pause. . . . or nothing worthwhile will catch up to you.
—Doug King, Poet

Roger von Oech (1986) states that one way to solve a problem is *not* to try to solve it. Just gather information and ideas from a wide range of sources and let the ideas develop toward a solution. What if we were to give students a major problem to work on throughout the term, giving them the direction, the time to gather information, and a chance to discover possible solutions themselves?

The ABC News production of "Common Miracles: The New American Revolution in Learning" focused on innovative school programs across the country. In one school, those students who "couldn't keep up" were not placed in specially grouped classes but instead were each given some 270 individually designed assignments to complete at their own pace and with assistance. Many of these assignments allowed them to come up with their own solutions or approaches. By completing these assignments, students could, possibly, finish three years of learning within one year.

Another school focused on higher-order thinking skills by using "incomplete teaching" and computers. Bill Blakemore, ABC-TV correspondent, stated that the students are intentionally led into frustration. They want to play the computer game, but when they ask the teacher for help, the teacher tells them everything they need to know is on the computer screen and walks away, allowing them to solve the task themselves. They fail at first but still work at solving the task because they *want* to solve it. Eventually most do succeed.

We want students to be able to recall knowledge or information to process or use it when needed. However, do we teach them *how* to remember? I can't recall ever teaching my students how to remember. (Must be educational amnesia!) Tony Buzan (1984), the author of several best-selling books on memory, talked about a variety of ways to improve one's memory. For example, he recommends

- making associations between specific facts and elements of a process and vivid colors, which can improve a person's memory as much as 50 percent (Richard III dressed in blood red would be an example of associative memory, or Edison in a yellow light bulb glow);

- imagining items as gigantic or miniature or bizarre; and

- associating items with a type of music, one of the five senses, movement, a number, or in sequence.

Do we teach students to visualize their success, to mentally focus on achieving? Most of us do not. The psychologist authors of *Beyond Strength*, commissioned by the U.S. Olympic Committee, stated, "We have found that Olympians who actually made the team were significantly more likely to use visualization than athletes who just missed" (Ungerleider and Golding 1992, 22). Many professional musicians use visualization to improve their playing and self-confidence. Why can't students? We can teach them to relax, to see themselves succeed, and to visualize their mistakes and how to correct them. Visualization can be a powerful tool for student success.

SOME POSSIBLE IN-SCHOOL ACTIVITIES

Renaming Students

Whatever the focus or theme of the class, a teacher can rename the students in that class according to the subject. For example, if the focus happens to be medieval history, each student might choose, or possibly select through a random drawing, a category (royalty, laborer, peasant, middle class, homeless, writer, performer, store owner, or minority) or choose an actual historic character from that time. The student then researches that character, sees through that character's eyes, behaves like that character while in class, and presents work from that character's perspective. Of course, each student should discuss that character with the rest of the class. The same could be done in science, literature, physical education, art, music, drama, and math.

Telling Tales

We know that stories, traditional folktales, and personal stories provide a unique and powerful way to involve students—especially at-risk students. Stories can provide structure, give direction, provide a release for emotions, reinforce morals and societal guidelines, give role models, and promote family—social values and positive relationships.

Have a student recite the lyrics to a popular or traditional song or nursery rhyme. The student then reveals the *true* story of how this song came to be or what the song *really* means. Shy students might sit in front of the room while the class interviews them about the story behind the song.

If you can seat the students in a circle, tell chain stories. One student (ideally a volunteer) or the group leader or the teacher begins a story about anything (maybe a chalkboard eraser, a car, an ant). Each person may have to keep telling for one minute or two. Or each person just adds a sentence to the story as it continues around the class, or maybe just a word. After the story has been "told out," students could

- summarize the story orally or in writing (there is no right or wrong version: just what the listener heard);

- create, orally or in writing, a new ending; or,

- with someone leading, discuss what they liked about the story, didn't like, and how to improve the story (not any one person's telling of it), paying attention to whether there was enough detail, dialogue, and good character description and whether the action was easy to follow.

Present or choose three objects—if they can be seen or held all the better—to a student. The student must then create a story that involves in some way all three objects. (The stranger the objects, the more fun!) Try telling tall tales, too.

Making Masks

Students love to make masks, and masks can be created out of many materials: cloth, paper bags, papier-mâché, feathers, cardboard, leather, wood, and more.

The masks created might represent a particular period or culture, or be personal masks. (A maskmaker might come to class to explain the history and meaning of masks and to demonstrate the art of mask-making. In one class, the students, under supervision, placed papier-mâché over each other's faces to make personal masks. (It was an amazing experience to observe the sensitivity and care they gave each other!) The student may paint or create an outer face representing how that student feels he or she is viewed by others and then design the inside of the mask to depict that student's inner feelings and thoughts. If there is good class bonding and trust, then perhaps the students will share what their personal masks specifically represent. They could also stage a performance with these masks.

Analyzing Pictures

Ask each student to draw a picture on a piece of paper of whatever first pops into that student's mind. It doesn't have to be a beautiful picture or a finished one. It might be representational, impressionistic, or abstract. On a separate piece of paper, the student then writes an analysis of that drawing: What is it? What does it represent to the student? What are the student's feelings about the drawing? What ideas or associations does it bring to mind? The teacher then gives the picture to someone else in the class. That person also analyzes it according to the four previous questions. After this, the entire class gets to see the picture and hear both analyses. (There is no correct or incorrect interpretation, just two points of view.)

Creating Images

I have used this activity in poetry and fiction-writing classes and in classes on movies, literature, historical figures, and interpersonal communication. Have each student choose a character in a picture, remember a specific character from a book or movie, or, possibly, join with another person in the room—sitting opposite that person. In complete quiet—no talking allowed—each student concentrates on that other character or person. Then, on paper, each student answers the following: What would this character or person be like as

- a body of water (temperature, depth, flow)?
- a light (color, intensity)?
- music (what kind)?
- a house (style, atmosphere, location)?
- an animal?

This then may be shared with the class, just with the teacher, or just with the person in class whom the student was observing.

Other Activities

Have each student

- research what each part of that student's name means and why the parents chose that name;
- write an account, fiction or fact, of how that student's parents met;
- write a letter of complaint, real or imagined, to a business or person;

- go back in time to interview a famous deceased person or to bring the class to the scene of a great historic event;

- write a real or fictional "Dear Abby" letter;

- exchange letters with someone else in class or in another class for a reply;

- play charades; or

- make up meanings for obscure words found in the dictionary.

On Fridays, in each class toward the end of the class period, hand each student a blank index card. Ask students to write on their cards

- any questions they have about the material studied, assignments, or process in class;

- how they are feeling about your teaching and their learning and why they feel that way;

- how they are doing with this class: concerns, feelings, comments; and

- other things they may choose to share that are affecting their learning.

Turning in the card blank is acceptable if the student can't or doesn't choose to complete it. The teacher, though, has provided another channel for feedback and communication. Whatever is written on the cards is confidential information. If the teacher wishes to discuss an issue mentioned, or to comment in return, that would be done personally or in a general way for the class, but not directed at any one student. (The teacher may ask students to write their names on the cards, or not.)

STUDENTS IN THE COMMUNITY

In order to acquire life skills, students must have the opportunity to explore the adult community and to become involved in any of a myriad of positive activities within the community throughout their school years. As Stephen Glenn (1990) noted in one of his workshops, "The compulsory education law specifies schools are to prepare young people to be responsible citizens: there's nothing about reading, writing, math in the law." Students learn responsibility, to be active community members, through personal participation and valued involvement. We should recognize that the most important student, indeed, human, need in life is to find meaning, purpose, and significance in today's world and in the future. Students experience fulfillment of these needs when they are understood, accepted, and affirmed in school and outside of school.

> I don't think the measure of a civilization is how tall its buildings are, but rather how well its people have learned to relate to their environment and to their fellow man.
>
> —Sun Bear of the Chippewa tribe

So in the future, schools must go beyond the school walls. They must provide times and ways for students to participate as future citizens in their local, state, national, and international communities.

Mentorships

In eighth grade or in high school, each student should have the experience of being paired with an adult mentor in that student's area of interest. (If necessary, two or three students might meet with the same mentor, but this makes the development of personal relationships difficult.) The student meets the mentor outside of the school building during the school day, or at other times convenient to the mentor. Together they plan a goal or project to accomplish. After this six- or ten-week experience, the student presents some type of display, project, or talk about what happened during this mentorship. Students have given presentations on whales, gardening, raising pigs, building rockets, photography, designing buildings, performing a surgical operation, and soccer skills. They keep a journal of their meetings, the evolution of the project, problems, and feelings.

Who better to train the staff on the use and range of computers than our students? Many of them know far more about and possess a much greater degree of understanding about computer technology than we do. Why shouldn't they become the teachers and we learn?

Community Service

Each middle school student could be expected—as part of the school curriculum—to participate in a community service experience. For a six-week period, four hours per week, the student either leaves during the school day or works the equivalent hours after school or on weekends in an agreed-upon volunteer situation in the community. One student might work in the video store across the street during the school day, another for the veterinarian after school; a third might spend two complete days on a weekend helping with the Special Olympics. In each instance, the student keeps a journal of experiences, feelings, changes in attitudes, and the meaning for that student of this volunteer experience.

Professor Roland S. Barth of Harvard University (1991) cited the example of students in Fairbanks, Alaska, adopting a shopping center, rather than a business adopting the classroom. The students went to the mall and each class adopted a store. Fourth-grade students went to the pet store, cleaned cages, fed animals, arranged shelves. Another grade set up displays at a variety store. Middle school students not only helped but were expected to learn about the various aspects of the retail business. In response to the students' goodwill, many stores in the shopping center began to volunteer to do things for the school.

Teens have worked on

- promoting awareness of safety and health issues from drunk driving to AIDS, drugs, and safe sex;
- developing community awareness of science and math;
- producing drama and arts concerts and programs for senior citizens;
- tutoring adult nonreaders;
- tutoring other students;
- training and working as peer counselors;
- developing and producing communication materials for the community about teen issues, views, needs, and problems;
- developing and hosting a radio series for young people or for the community;
- cleaning up waterways and educating the community about pollution;
- removing graffiti and helping to prevent more;
- repairing and maintaining the housing and/or yards for the poor and elderly;
- serving on community committees;
- teaching and helping at local religious organizations and events;
- tutoring and assisting migrant peoples;
- organizing multicultural events to effect greater community understanding;
- studying garbage and community recycling needs and ways to help;
- coaching children's sports teams;
- organizing dance, arts, and physical fitness programs;
- creating and arranging community events;
- organizing youth talent shows for community performances;
- looking for small businesses that may need help for short time periods;
- working in hospitals and in retirement and nursing homes;
- creating, updating, and publishing a teen directory of emergency services and how to use them;

- collecting and distributing clothing for those in need;
- adopting a park;
- surveying food and nutrition practices in the schools, in the community, and among children and publishing the results and suggestions;
- organizing and holding a series of public teen-parent meetings and issue discussions;
- joining the Big Brother/Big Sister program;
- working in a pediatrics ward or preschool;
- helping with political organizations or policy groups;
- assisting families experiencing serious illness;
- organizing and training a group of young people to speak to various community groups on issues concerning children and teens;
- repairing bicycles and other sports equipment;
- creating bird or animal sanctuaries;
- developing a beautification plan for a specific area or the city as a whole: planting shrubs, flowers, and trees;
- planting and tending vegetable gardens, using the produce for those in need, especially children;
- and more!

The state, city, school district, and schools should establish annual awards, certificates, and recognition celebrations for specific projects and for young people who have contributed to their communities.

REFERENCES

Armstrong, Thomas. 1992. "Awakening the Genius of the Child." Presented at the Education 2000 Conference, Eugene, OR, July.

Barker, L. R. Edwards, C. Gaines, K. Gladney, and E. Holley. 1981. "An Investigation of Proportional Time Spent in Various Communication Activities by College Students." *Journal of Applied Communication Research* 8: 101-9.

Barth, Roland S. 1991. "Restructuring Schools: Some Questions for Teachers and Principals." *Phi Delta Kappan* (October).

Buzan, Tony. 1984. *Use Your Perfect Memory*. New York: E. P. Dutton.

Chira, Susan. l993. "Arts Backers Try to Save Classes." *Eugene Register-Guard* (February 15): 6A.

"Common Miracles: The New American Revolution in Learning." 1993. ABC News.

deBono, Edward. l989. "Creative and Lateral Thinking" workshop. Portland, OR, December 8.

Doyle, Denis P., and Susan Pimentel. l993. "What's in and What's out in '93." *Education Week* (January 13): 43.

Gardner, Howard. *Frames of Mind*. New York: Basic Books, 1983.

Glasser, William. 1992. "Quality School Curriculum." *Phi Delta Kappan* (May): 690-94.

Glenn, Stephen. l991. "Changing Paradigms for Youth" workshop. Eugene, OR, October 11.

————. 1990. "Developing Capable People" workshop. Portland, OR, March.

"The Harvard Education Letter." March 1988.

Hillman, James. 1979. "A Note on Story." *Parabola IV*: 59-66.

"Just Do It!" l993. *Newsweek* (March 29): 123-28.

Littlebird, Larry. 1991. "Learning to Listen." *Coyote Gathers His People Newsletter* (Fall): 3.

Marzano, Robert. 1992. "Changing Instruction and Assessment." Education 2000 Conference. Eugene, OR, July.

McKenzie, Jamieson. 1987. "Making Change in Education." In *Skills for the 21st Century*. New York: Wilkerson.

Rubinstein, Robert E. l991. "Telling Tales with At-Risk Students." *FL Educator* (Summer): 4-6.

————. 1986. "Traveling Tales." *Friendly Exchange* (Febrary): 19.

Steil, L. K. 1978. "Listen My Students . . . and You Shall Learn." *Towards Better Teaching* 11 (Fall).

Stern, Deborah. 1992. "Structure and Spontaneity: Teaching with the Student at Risk." *English Journal* (October): 49-53.

Sternberg, Robert J., and Todd I. Lubart. 1991. "Creating Creative Minds." *Phi Delta Kappan* (April): 608-14.

"Tom McCall Awards for Community Service," 1991. KATU-TV and Fred Meyer Stores. Portland, OR.

Ungerleider, Steven, and Jacqueline M. Golding. 1992. *Beyond Strength: Psychological Profiles of Olympic Athletes*. Dubuque, IA: Wm. C. Brown.

Varney, Sheldon S. 1990. "Understanding Cultural Diversity Can Improve Intercultural Interactions." *NASSP Bulletin* (October): 89-94.

von Oech, Roger. 1986. *A Kick in the Seat of the Pants*. New York: Perennial Library.

Why Do We Test?

> *We live in a society of quick response. Einstein was slow speaking and slow to use linguistic writing. Would he have passed a national exam?*
> —Dr. Thomas Armstrong, Educator

TESTING AS A FORM OF ASSESSMENT

Why do we give students tests? As teachers, we might answer: "We give students tests to find out what they've learned and to give them grades in that subject or class." These tests may also, as in the case of national testing or standardized testing, determine the educational future of a child.

According to a 1992 report from the Association for Childhood Education International on standardized testing, such testing

- causes children to feel more pressure and results in a lowering of self-esteem;

- does not provide useful information about helping individual children yet may influence important decisions about a child's education;

- often results in the harmful tracking and labeling of children;

- forces teachers to focus valuable learning time preparing children to take these tests, resulting in a tightly restricted—rather than expanded—curriculum; and

- does not encourage cooperative learning and problem solving.

The report also notes that standardized tests are not designed "to assess educational performance, but to help determine placement—first in the military and later in overcrowded colleges and universities" (9). The media, however, and the American public's appetite for accountability have made these tests into something never intended by those who designed them. (The same is true for the so-called IQ test, which was not originally designed to test a child's intelligence.)

So we must beware of what groups make up these tests and for what specific—maybe political or religious—purposes. We cannot just accept these tests and their results because they are supposedly "national tests" or "for the good of education."

In addition to this is the problem children encounter when taking these tests. As Sylvia Sherry, a well-respected special education teacher at Roosevelt Middle School in Eugene, observed, standardized tests, which in many cases are used as final examinations for classes, are too long for students, especially those who are slower or in the middle schools, to sit through. The number of pages and amount of information can be overwhelming; the student reacts with "How am I ever going to do this?" Sherry believes that we need positive methods, built into the testing process and also practiced by those administering the tests, to help keep the students focused.

The use and abuse of these standardized tests is one prime example of how carried away we in education and the general public can become with pencil and paper testing. How much do we rely on this type of testing in our classrooms, and how often do we use these test scores as the main way to evaluate a student's overall performance?

We know that to learn a skill you first must experience failure. When a child sets out to learn to ride a bicycle, we expect that child to fall several, if not many, times before mastering that skill. The same applies to a young athlete learning to bat or to shoot a basketball. For some strange reason, however, we expect students to do well on tests—all tests—from the beginning. We penalize them heavily if they "fall off the bike," or "miss the shot."

If, however, teachers believe that learning should be a positive, success-oriented process and experience for students, then we must give a wide variety of types of tests and use test results with great care. For, according to the student-centered approach, tests should show how well that student has learned, what he or she needs to learn, and how well that student can take that particular test. Tests, then, should be a positive learning experience, not a pass or fail one, for the student.

Testing should be only one of the tools used to help the student and the teacher assess how well that young person has learned over a period of time. Some people simply do not do well on tests, especially very important tests such as midterms and finals, which require that the student ingest and repeat huge amounts of information. (Outside of the classroom, where in our society and in real life does a person have one comprehensive "final" test that determines his or her failure at that job? It seldom happens. Then why do we subject children to this?) Because students become ill or do not perform well on major examinations does not mean they haven't learned or that they cannot make practical use of that information (if that information is worth using and remembering) and those skills. Therefore, testing should be only one of several ways to evaluate student success, along with written papers, classwork, attendance, projects, and so on.

The unasked question that screams for a response is, if our ultimate goal is to teach this child to read, how does the "C-" further that end? The answer is plain. It doesn't. . . . Grades are arbitrary at best. Most teachers could rank most students in "A" through "D" categories at the end of the first week or two. . . . There is no good to be gotten from the process of consistently pointing out a person's shortcomings. We need to find and encourage every person's individual competencies. That is our job. That is why we are teachers. (Blynt 1992, 67)

We narrowly define "intelligence and learning" as the ability of a child to read and write at a certain grade level at a certain time in that child's life that we adults arbitrarily determine. If the child performs well, he or she is "word smart"—that's all. Based on the child's performance, we begin labeling and tracking that child, especially if the child does not meet this grade "definition."

We need an assessment process that shows us what each person knows and how each person can apply that knowledge. Again, as assessment tools for measuring individual progress, standardized tests have many drawbacks:

- Tests do not recognize or take into consideration student background and ethnic heritage. For example, 75 percent of the kindergartners in Los Angeles do not speak English. Bettie Sing Luke, in her multicultural workshop, told of a group of high school Asian students new to this country who in one year learned English well enough to score average on the IQ test. The counselor told them that average was not good enough to consider college. (Luke 1992)

- According to Howard Gardner, students apply seven different types of intelligences to learning. Written tests can evaluate only two of these, linear and logical, and seldom do an adequate job of even this.

- Tests result in unjustified comparisons and competition among students when we know that each progresses at his or her own individual pace.

- Tests do not allow individual expression, opinion, creativity, or achievement. Students risk failure and "punishment" if they dare try to express themselves.

- Tests do not tell us what students have learned, only what they may *not* have learned.

- One standardized test score can make us doubt a child with whom we've been working for six months or an entire year.

- Any test should be a learning tool, not an instrument of personal failure. National examinations and "final" tests just further expose students who have difficulties performing well on written tests. How would Marcel Proust with his bent for run-on sentences, or Ernest Hemingway with his brief sentence patterns have passed a national test? Leonardo da Vinci wrote backwards, had dyslexia, and was a horrible speller. He would have been a test failure.

In Indiana, a high school teacher explained to parents that he gave pretests but never discussed or analyzed the results of these tests with the students. In this way, the students would not have an "advantage" on the actual test, he stated. A parent asked him: "Where is the learning then if you operate in this way?" The teacher replied, "I must do it this way to prepare them for college. This is the way college teachers teach." Whereupon, the parent asked again, "So if college teachers teach so poorly, then you should teach as poorly in high school?"

Our methods of grading are also faulty. The almighty bell curve creates a situation where half the students *must* fail or lose. If they do too well on an exam, many teachers adjust the bell curve to make certain that half fail. Why would we do this to young people—to children trying to learn?

National testing is big business and costly to schools. According to Dr. Pamela Aschbacher (1992), our public schools spend more than $100 million annually on direct testing costs, more than $800 million on indirect testing costs, and more than $20 million pupil school days on administering these tests. It would be unreasonable to expect that these testing services would want to see testing reduced or reconsidered in our schools. Do these testing services lobby, exert pressure on so-called national education studies, on school districts, on states to ensure the stability of this lucrative field? In many instances, we are not even certain what these tests are determining about student learning and the effectiveness of our schools. Many have been shown to be biased in favor of white males from urban and suburban areas, primarily in the eastern United States. Yet we spend the money and subject students to them anyway—while the public anxiously waits and judges teachers and schools by the results.

In one survey, 300 of 400 students interviewed expressed their dislike for school or had problems with school. Student attitude certainly affects testing and assessment (Glenn 1992). How do tests encourage most students to enjoy learning, to feel successful, and to work toward individual goals? After all, isn't this the purpose of learning? Of teaching?

PREPARING STUDENTS FOR A TEST

Taking tests is a learned skill, but few students have received instructions in taking specific types of tests. We know that students learn at different rates and in different ways. They also prepare for tests differently. In most cases, students have no sense of time passing and do not plan for studying for a test. So they end up in a panic, cramming the night before. This can be avoided with some help from the teacher.

- At least a week in advance, inform students of the date of the test and what type of test it will be. Note what material the test will cover.

- Encourage students to use visualization, to "see" the material or use imagery to associate the material to be remembered.

- Daily, write on the blackboard the number of days left until the test. Students' lives are very busy and very complicated. They need your help to prepare them and keep them on task.

- Each day, you might mention what students should be studying at that time. In this way, they can review small amounts of material daily and avoid the last-minute cramming.

- Suggest that they make sure they have all the class notes and have done the readings.

- Suggest that they review any assignments, past tests, or worksheets that might help them study for this test. They should note especially what problems they had on previous work and how to remedy those problems, or have the opportunity to consult you or other students.

- One or two days before the test, take time in class to review the material covered in class. This review will help students who have been absent. It will very likely, for many students, bring the material together in some comprehensive, cohesive way they can understand: the "Oh, I see now!" enlightenment.

- Allow students time to question you about the material so they can clarify their understanding. (We shouldn't be focused on covering amounts of material as much as making certain the students understand the material covered in meaningful, relevant ways.)

- In your review, you might pose some sample questions in the form they will appear on the test.

At any rate, let the students know what type of test, such as essay, they will be taking.

CREATING A TEST

Even if students happen to pass a test, studies show that in a short span of time they forget most of the information studied. Stephen Glenn (1990) mentioned in one of his workshops that a friend tested a group of high school students. In May these students all passed a high school comprehensive, informa- tion recall exam for graduation. When they were tested again in July on the same material, 90 percent did not pass. What is the purpose of a test unless we do our best to make it a learning tool? The goal should be that students learn and retain useful information or processes, not just that they do well on the test. Teachers can create more effective tests in a variety of ways.

Using open-ended questions, what Stephen Glenn calls capstone questions, allows the student to determine the personal value of what's been studied and reveals the student's understanding of the material. (Capstone questions might be: "How might you apply what we've studied to your life, or to the world?" "Why do *you* think the king acted this way? How might a different reaction have changed the course of the events?") The inquiry process allows the teacher to gain a better insight into how well the student understands the material.

With any of the questions on short-answer tests, there might be a place for the student to write in a better answer than those suggested. This encourages thinking, logic, and assembling supporting evidence for an answer. The student should have the opportunity to explain why the answer offered is better. If the student demonstrates the understanding, the thinking, logic and evidence, then give that student double or triple the points! This is what we want—students thinking creatively and critically!

Tests that allow the student or a group of students to collect information and then use that information to solve a specific problem demonstrates understanding and learning.

Plan to give students the time and opportunity to answer the questions successfully. Timed tests put a great deal of pressure on those who know the material but just work slowly.

Develop questions based on what the students need to know, understand, and use. Testing on trivia does not help students make the connections that make information meaningful.

Give clear, easy-to-understand written and oral directions. For example, if you ask a student to do something "clockwise," remember that at home some students may have no clocks with hands, only digital ones. In class, students often face the clock.

Most tests strongly favor white males. Use nonstereotypic examples: names, references, and verbs that also refer to females and minorities.

If you have students from other ethnic groups who were not born in the United States, they may have problems with references. If you mention a cup and want them to match it with a saucer, what happens if they have never seen or don't use cups and saucers. By the year 2000, one in three students in our schools will be people of color.

TEACHING STUDENTS HOW TO TAKE SPECIFIC TESTS

We must keep in mind that written tests are only one way—maybe accounting for two intelligences of the seven—for students to show what they have learned. Some of these written tests include *multiple choice, matching, fill-in-the-blanks, true-or-false, sentence* or *essay, open-note, group tests,* and *student-created tests.*

On any test, the first thing students should do is read through the entire test *before* answering any questions. This will allow students to understand what must be answered, to determine how much time to allot for the different questions, and very often to find information in other parts of the test that may help answer questions or trigger ideas for answers. (I often purposely plant helpful information throughout the test to encourage students to learn to use the test.)

When taking tests students should, in most cases, move through the entire test, immediately answering the questions they readily know. They should avoid getting "stuck" on figuring out the answer to a single question. After they have answered as many questions as they know, students should return to those questions that posed the most difficulty for them. Students may find they gain helpful insight, information, or understanding as a result of going through the entire test first, then returning to those "difficult" questions.

Multiple-Choice Tests

A little guidance on multiple-choice tests helps students approach the answer choices. First, test-takers should read *all* the answers because they must select the *best* one of these. With most good multiple-choice tests of, let's say, four choices, one choice is ridiculous and can easily be eliminated. A second choice is also often not related to the question. So there are usually two possible choices, or a 50-50 chance of choosing the correct answer. If the student has studied, the correct answer may be immediately apparent. If not, the student can use the understanding gained to lessen the odds of choosing incorrectly. The student has also gained some knowledge about the process of making choices in general.

True-or-False Tests

A true-or-false test usually depends on the wording of the statements. If the statement reads "Every fish swims in the ocean," then even if students lack the specific knowledge, they should know that the statement is false because it uses an extreme, all-inclusive word: *every*. If words such as *everyone, no one, nothing, none, all,* or *everything* are used in a statement, 99 percent of the time that statement is false. One of the most difficult things to teach about this type of test is not to read more into the statement than is there. The student must learn to take the statement at face value and not think of all the far-out possible alternatives the statement might include. Practice with these types of statements helps the student prepare.

Matching Tests

Matching tests again rely on the *best* matches or choices. Students should read both columns of possible matching answers to see what is there. Can some answers be used twice? Are there more answers than can be used (which means that some answers will not be used)? Are the directions clear as to where and how to record the matches?

With a test like this, students should first use all the answers they are sure about, crossing those off. Then, they can move on to the rest. In this way, the student has reduced the number of possible answers.

Fill-in-the-Blanks Tests

Fill-in-the-blanks tests can be some of the most difficult, and the teacher should be well aware of this. With these types of tests, we ask the student to read the teacher's mind: What does the teacher want written in that blank space? Often, the phrasing of the statement incorporating the blanks, the punctuation, or the possible answers are not clear. Does the blank stand for one word? Can a phrase be put into the blank? Is there a blank per word? Must the student use the exact term, or can the answer be paraphrased? It's best if the test is a series of distinct sentences or short paragraphs. Long passages with blanks usually seem jumbled and confusing.

Probably the best type of fill-in-the-blanks test, which reinforces the specific terms and their usage, is one that lists a pool of words to be used in the test. In this way, the teacher can control the responses, and the student understands more clearly and uses the specific terms learned.

Short Answer or Essay Tests

With this type of test, the student should have the ability to assimilate information and the main points in order to explain or defend a position or answer a significant question about the material covered. The student has the opportunity to show understanding and insight. The teacher, however, must have a good degree of flexibility. If the student expresses an opinion, explains it well, and uses examples, then the teacher needs the open-mindedness to accept that opinion and the effort put forth even though it may not be the answer the teacher expected or wanted. Thinking, enthusiasm, and process are far more important than parroting information. The process and technique of answering essay questions should be practiced in class on the blackboard for all to see, copy, and understand.

Students should approach this type of test by first carefully reading the question to determine what is actually being asked. The next step is to quickly brainstorm by jotting down on scrap paper any information or ideas. From these jottings should come, if there is time, a quick rough draft, and then a polished draft.

In general, students should learn to answer the test question by restating that question at the beginning of the answer. If the question is, "Why do dogs pant?" the answer should begin, "Dogs pant because . . . ." If a question requires a series of answers—"Give three reasons why the United States entered World War II"—it's important that students do not fall into the listing or run-on sentence trap. "The three reasons we entered World War II are . . . ," is the beginning of a listing sentence, which usually leads to a run-on and tangled sentence and does not allow for any detailed explanation. It is better to isolate each reason in a separate sentence, yet still keep the restatement of the question as part of the answer: "There are several reasons the United States entered World War II. One reason is . . . . " This type of response allows for clearer, more detailed answers and avoids run-on sentences.

Open-Note Tests

We already mentioned, with Stephen Glenn's example, that asking students to rote memorize great amounts of information for a test is virtually worthless and does little to promote learning or retention of the information.

If students have taken a great many notes, have printed materials, quizzes, and homework, you might consider an open-note test.

For this test, students need to organize their notes in a meaningful way that will make the notes useful. In going back and forth through their notes, searching for the information and answers, the students do, in effect, study all the material. Therefore, they learn more than just what is needed for the test answers. This also takes the pressure off those students who do not retain large chunks of facts well but who do understand the material and, with those facts in front of them, can answer questions. It's important that the questions asked seem relevant and worthwhile to the students and are not questions that ask the student to find some inconsequential reference in the notes.

Group Tests

For a group of three to six or eight, you might assign tasks to complete using concepts and information taught. You observe who leads and contributes, and who doesn't. Once the task is completed, a short oral or written quiz might follow on what the group accomplished and how well the students felt they worked together. In addition, each person in the group might be assessed on individual follow-through or completion of specific assigned tasks.

Oral Tests

Informal oral testing, of course, can and should happen daily in class and should consist of asking individual students about the material and ideas presented in class. The trick is to question students in a random, nonthreatening way and yet, over a period of one or two days, have each student in class respond to a question. A teacher should try not to allow the overzealous students to dominate and should gently encourage those who are reluctant to answer. At the end of the period, the teacher might make some quick notes on how well each student answered questions during that class.

An oral quiz can involve students responding either orally or on paper. This type of test can be used to evaluate listening and interpretation skills.

Student-Created Tests

An interesting way to evaluate student understanding of materials and ideas as well as what the students perceive as significant is to ask the students to make up their own quizzes.

- Each student might create two or three questions to contribute to a class test.

- Each student might make up an individual quiz, complete with directions, focusing on what that student feels is important to know or understand. That same student can answer the questions, or others might take the student's test.

- You might include student questions on a test you make up.

The students receive points or an evaluation based on the clarity of the questions and/or on successfully completing a student-created quiz. Students value this type of quiz because they feel ownership in the process.

Projects or Presentations

Students with varying abilities and ways of learning can demonstrate what they've learned and what is significant to them, through a project or presentation. For a piece of literature, a movie, or a section of history, a student might do a drawing, write poems or a story, perform a skit (maybe one that demonstrates a math or science concept), create models, make a video, write original jokes, or draw cartoons. (How great it is to see students actually have fun with the material and ideas—to play, parody, and find humor—to be creatively thinking and using what's been taught!)

For presentations about mythologies around the world in my Myths and Legends class, or on various sports in my Sports: Then and Now class, I ask the student audience to take notes on the student presentations. (Usually these are just the notes the student speaker writes on the board. I will "direct" the notes to be written on the board if necessary.) After all the presentations have been completed, we have an open-note quiz on the important ideas and facts in the material presented.

Interviews

One way to assess a student's understanding of the material and concepts is to informally interview that student or a small group of students. Perhaps this interview can take place during class, before or after school, or at some other time. It is best to limit the time for such tests to between five and ten minutes for individual student meetings, and ten to fifteen minutes for a two- to four-person group. Food with the interview always helps.

With this approach, the student will, ideally, be more relaxed and open, ready to share what's been learned in a more personal way. The teacher can revise questions to focus on that particular student's ability level, interests, and way of perceiving the material and concepts and can do so in a problem-solving, creative way. This would be especially helpful with slower learners and with talented and gifted learners.

Humor Helps

Very few people do not suffer from some degree of test anxiety. Sometimes, that anxiety becomes so great that people cannot function or perform nearly as well as they are capable of doing. (I had an experience on a comprehensive bachelor's degree exam on which I answered every question accurately, but the sentences were incomprehensible. Yet I had the top scores in my expository writing class at that college. Before this test, I was physically ill just from the prospect of taking one test that was of such importance.)

If you have a background in relaxation techniques or learn some, then these can be taught to students. If not, laughter releases some tension and helps students to relax.

I often make up strange titles for my tests: "The Ice Cold Quiz" for a Viking test, "The Knight Day Quiz" for medieval times, or "The Over-the-Hill Quiz" or "You'd-Better-Pass-This-One Quiz."

I slip in humorous, silly answers to questions:

"Were" of "were-wolf" means
a. rabbit   b. rock musician   c. man   d. tiger

A page was someone who
a. was 18   b. came before a squire   c. was ripped out of a book

On matching tests, an answer or two is ridiculous and, I hope, funny. Not only does the funny answer relax the student, but it also builds confidence. The student knows that one answer is definitely wrong.

DURING THE TEST

A teacher cannot assume that the written or oral test directions are clear for each student. Students as individual learners receive information in many different ways. Some do better with oral instructions, others with written ones, and still others must ask questions. Teachers must be open to all of these channels of communication.

So that students will feel comfortable asking me questions, I get out from behind my desk. The desk is a barrier, a formidable one for students. I walk among the students to offer help and encouragement. Shy students can gain my attention and help, and I notice if a student is working successfully or is very frustrated (a little hint can give that student direction and confidence). Moving among the students also reduces attempts at cheating.

If I feel a student is talking to another, or looking at another's paper, I usually give a low-key warning first—for I could be wrong. I tell them before the test begins: "If I think you're talking or looking at someone else's paper, I will give you one warning. The next time, you lose the test, receive a zero, and there are no make-ups." It's simply a matter of natural consequences once students have been warned.

SCORING TESTS

Unless a test is flawed, whatever a student earns on a test should be the test score. On some of my spelling-proof-reading tests, students have scored 150 percent or even 225 percent. There is no reason for the traditional mind-set of 100 percent as an end limit. (After all, we do have test scores, for example, of 24 correct out of 40, and SAT scores in the 1400s.) If the student earns a score of 260, that's great! That's what I want. That student has done a wonderful job studying for and succeeding on this test!

Why would a good teacher downgrade test scores because the students have done too well? Isn't that what we want students to do? Don't we want them to succeed? If every one of my students scored in the 90s out of 100 percent on my tests, that would be fine!

By the same reasoning, it isn't fair to the student for the teacher to create trick questions on a test for the purpose of showing the students how stupid they are, how much they don't know. What's the purpose in that? It's simply a put-down of the student, a deterrent to success and enjoying learning, and a power trip for the teacher.

USING THE TEST AS A LEARNING TOOL

One of the most, if not *the* most, important parts of giving a test is the review of the correct answers on that test. How else does a student learn from the test?

With many quizzes, I collect the tests and redistribute them to other students, making certain a student does not receive his or her own test. I ask the students not to reveal whose tests they are grading. True, to a few students, this process could be embarrassing, but the need to understand *why* an answer is right or wrong as well as how other students arrived at the answer outweighs this in my opinion. The "why" is the essential learning element of the quiz. We then go over the questions orally, discussing how those questions probably should have been answered and reviewing the correct answers.

During the review, the students have a chance to ask me about parts of the test. If I cannot adequately explain to them why an answer is correct, or if the same problems keep recurring in the answers to a particular question, then the test may be flawed, and the students should not be penalized for their answers to that question.

The end result is that the students have explanations for the correct answers and the tests have been corrected.

Students should keep these tests and use them to study for future tests. Show them how to review past quizzes to determine what type of questions caused them problems and why they lost points. I do not usually give make-up tests. If a student does not pass a quiz, usually with 70 percent or better, then that student is to recopy the entire quiz, answering the questions correctly and in complete sentences. This quiz can then be used to study for future quizzes. The goal is to reinforce the material covered.

If we are to use testing as a part of education, then let's make it a positive learning experience and a learning tool for the student.

GRADES AND EVALUATIONS

Why do we need to give grades to any student under the age of sixteen? Studies tell us that by the age of fourteen, 87 percent of young people have contemplated suicide and that suicide, if we include suspicious fatal accidents, is the leading cause of teen deaths in our country. The most frequent reason given for teens contemplating suicide is that they do not feel valued by others or good about themselves. Grades certainly don't help the situation for the vast majority of the students.

Anyone reading a student's grade, for example, an A, should understand that the grade does not mean that this is an "A student" but that, at this time with this particular teacher, the student is doing what that teacher happens to consider "A work."

There's something wrong when a teacher espouses a system that gives a student with an 87 percent average a B because it's not "really an A." Why wouldn't you raise the student's grade, reward rather than penalize the student? We're not dealing with systems. We're dealing with people—young people.

Previously, I've mentioned a number of ways to evaluate or assess student progress other than written tests. *Evaluation* implies a comprehensive approach, looking at the wide variety of ways a student has learned and progressed as well as ways a particular student can best continue to improve and learn successfully.

If we accept, as we should, that learning is progressive, that the student does not instantly absorb and master the subject matter and skills in a particular class, then any value placed on tests should be progressively more weighted, too. If we must give "tests," then tests during the latter part of the term should be valued more than those in the earlier part of the term.

Portfolios

Keeping some type of portfolio containing samples of work throughout the term on each student in a class helps with evaluation. However, here again, the focus often is on mainly the student's written work. But a portfolio might also include notes about any informal discussions with that student and about that student's participation, project or demonstration, behavior, effort to contribute or work better, changes in attitude, group involvement, and contributions. With such information, the portfolio gives a much clearer picture for evaluating a student's progress and work.

A possible alternative to the portfolio, which I've used for many years is a large index card for each student in each class. On this card, I record test scores and make specific comments—using abbreviations—about each assignment (content, writing, spelling, punctuation, creativity), participation, behavior, doing work on time, special needs, and more. The student is welcome to see this card at any time and can read it with me to get an overview of how he or she is doing. We can discuss the card together. When parents come in and want to know how their child is doing, I take out the index card and show them.

Goal Sheets

If students have prepared goal sheets at the beginning of the term and, preferably, several times during the term, use these to evaluate progress toward those goals. The teacher might write an evaluation that includes reasons for progress or lack of it. The student might also write a self-assessment, including reasons for success or lack of progress. Both of these statements could be sent to parents.

Parent Conferences

The teacher might arrange for a parent conference about each student in class. Examples of student work, the index card or the portfolio should be on hand to show the parents. Consider giving the student the responsibility for conducting this meeting to review that his or her work. After all, the student has the responsibility for learning.

Written Progress Reports

For twenty years, Roosevelt teachers produced written evaluations every six weeks for each student in class. Each teacher designed the evaluation to fit the specific class taught.

My evaluation for "Myths and Legends" course included whether the student received credit or an incomplete, a brief description of the class content and expectations, and then specifically what the student accomplished and how the student might improve.

The student has received _____ Credit _____ Incomplete for this course.

In "Myths and Legends," we studied the ancient Greeks and Norse people as well as medieval tales of the Britons, tales from America, and tales from Native Americans.

Each student was expected to complete the assignments and writings, pass the quizzes, and participate in class.

Quizzes:
(70% is passing)_____

Question Sheets:_____
Letter to the Gods: _____

Original Tall Tale or
Medieval Tale: _____

In General: _____

I would write phrases or sentences on the evaluation. I could also tailor the evaluation to the individual student and addressed the comments to the student, not to the parents. The "In General" category allowed me to comment about participation, behavior, attitude, attendance, progress, and needs, and make recommendations.

The drawback with this type of evaluation is, of course, the time involved. Time and teacher effort must be weighed against the benefit of this personal evaluation to the student.

Computerized Evaluations

A method between grade reports and full written evaluations might be the computerized evaluations. With these, the teacher can indicate a symbol that represents the student's progress during the term. An S might represent super progress; G, good progress; A, adequate; B, below expectations; U, unsatisfactory; and NC, no credit for this class. Therefore, a slow student or student who has problems might receive an S if he or she has made a super effort to complete all the work, improve participation, and boost the quality of work—even though the work is not "A quality." A student who should be, but isn't, doing the quality of work he or she has demonstrated in previous classes might receive a B or U even though the work would have typically received a typical B grade.

A wide variety of comments with accompanying numbers might be listed so that the teacher can choose two or three appropriate comments to accompany the letter given:

#27—Positive Attitude

#59—More Participation Needed

#78—Overall Average: 90-95%

#22—Study More for Tests

#33—Creative and Innovative

#99—Wonderful Project!

I find the problem with computer evaluations is that, often, what I want to say to a specific student is not among the list of comments available. However, I can come a lot closer with this type of evaluation than I can by simply giving an arbitrary grade that conveys little specific appreciation of effort and gives no guidance in direction.

REFERENCES

Armstrong, Thomas. 1992. "Awakening the Genius of the Child" workshop. Education 2000 Conference, Eugene, OR, July.

Aschbacher, Pamela. 1992. "Alternative Assessment" workshop. Education 2000 Conference, Eugene, OR, July.

Association for Childhood Education International. 1992. "The Oregon Educational Act for the 21st Century." *Oregon Education* (April): 9.

Blynt, Ruth Ann. 1992. "The Sticking Place: Another Look at Grades and Grading." *English Journal* (October): 66-68.

Glenn, Stephen. 1990. "Developing Capable People" workshop. Portland, OR, March.

Kindred, Leslie W. 1981. *The Middle School Curriculum*. Boston: Allyn & Bacon.

Luke, Bettie Sing. 1992. Multicultural workshop. Roosevelt Middle School. Eugene, OR, April.

Miller, Patrick W., and Harley E. Erickson. 1985. *Teacher-Written Student Tests*. Washington, DC: National Education Association.

Sale, Larry L. *Introduction to Middle School Teaching*. 1979. Toronto: Charles E. Merrill.

The Positive Parent Connection

Parents respect school personnel who return that respect. . . .
They want to be equal partners with schools in the
rearing of their children.

—Jane C. Lindle
"What Do Parents Want from Students and Teachers?"

As a parent of three teenagers and as a middle school teacher, I have a chance to see my children and students, teaching and schools, through two perspectives.

As a parent, I want my children to have the best possible school experience. Their quality of life in the next century, in a world of uncertainty and growing socioeconomic gaps, largely depends on their doing well in school both academically and socially. There are school policies I don't agree with and those who I don't feel are quality teachers for my children.

As a teacher, I encounter hundreds of students a day in classes and around the school. When I teach, I try to use materials and techniques to meet the wide variety of learning styles and abilities of my students. However, I realize that I can't and don't reach every student effectively. My students bring a host of family, health, and other personal problems to school, and these affect their concentration, ability, and success in learning. I can't possibly know or deal with each student's range of personal problems. It's just too much; I don't have the resources, energy, or time.

The difficulty I've encountered with this dual role and dual perception is that I walk a tightrope between the caring parent and the professional teacher. When these roles conflict, the parent role, by and large, takes precedence. (There have been several instances when I knew that a teacher was not effective. I contacted my children's adviser-counselors to tell them that I did not want my child to be in that teacher's class.) I hope, though, that the teacher in me remains

and will remain influential enough to give me the sensitivity to work with my children's teachers in positive ways.

TODAY'S FAMILY

As a teacher, if I do want to help a child more and do want to find out more about a student's family, whom do I contact? The family today is often a conundrum: Who's related to whom and who's responsible for the child?

Lisa Graff, in her article "Parents Deserve the Blame," recounted her frustrations while teaching and her reasons for leaving teaching: "The most critical problem in the public school system is parents' own failure or unwillingness to control their child's behavior. . . . Teachers are expected to know how to control students' behavior in the classroom even if no parent can control them at home" (1991, 1B). She noted that in one year in the state of Maryland, parents or guardians voluntarily placed almost 500 children in foster care; another 700 children were simply abandoned by their parents. This didn't happen when I was a child.

Parents do need to take a more active role in their children's education. However, according to Graff, many students wish even more that their parents would take an interest in them as people first.

Today, with so much changing so quickly and such a degree of confusion in the minds of young people, it becomes even more vital that parents—and teachers—take an interest in students as people. If we take a moment to think back to our own school days, when most of us did have a two-parent family unit and extended family nearby, how much did our parents or close relatives support us in school? How did they relate to us as people? As students, what did we wish to change about the communication between our parents and ourselves?

Whatever factors we feel should have been different in our family relations when we were young are largely the same factors—only more so—that concern today's young people. Most of today's young people do not have strong family support. Only 26 percent of our students live in traditional two-parent families with their biological parents. The divorce rate stands at 50 percent. There are 12 million single-parent families.

Since the 1960s and, more recently, with the "me" generation, a continuing deemphasis on family and family obligations has occurred. As a result, our children are often left to fend for themselves. The title of Bernard Gavzer's *Parade* article—"What Is a Family?"—reflects this phenomenon. "Experts cite grim statistics on divorce, teenage pregnancy, incest, single parents, unwed couples, and abandonment" (1992, 14). The teenager's cry, "Please take notice of me as a person. Consider my needs and the parental support I must have," goes unheeded.

One-quarter of the children born today are born to unwed mothers. Half of these children will spend portions of their lives in single-parent families. Nearly half of all the families headed by mothers with children under eighteen live below the poverty line. In the past fifteen years, the number of mothers working outside the home has jumped 50 percent. Many children live in families with drug-abuse problems and are abused or neglected themselves.

In a recent survey, parents were surprised to find that the drug of choice among teenagers is alcohol and that six million teens drink regularly. How can parents be aware of this when a typical parent spends less then fifteen minutes each day communicating in a positive way with his or her child?

Gavzer's article goes on to note that strong families have two factors in common. These families protect their children and nurture them to grow to be valued members of society, and these families are committed to caring for their elderly members. All strong families, despite race, religion, wealth, and culture, are guided by these two powerful principles. Such families seem to be in the minority today.

WHAT DO PARENTS WANT FROM YOU?

Jane C. Lindle (1989), a former principal, noted that parents don't want school people to be "professional," presenting the cold, efficient, business approach in dealing with them.

What parents want most is to see and feel that school people care for their children, care about their children's personal happiness and success. Especially with the pressures of today's daily life on parents and on children, parents need our support, our help in any way that we can give it to them.

Parents need scheduled times, and enough time, to meet with us. Allotting fifteen minutes per parent visit doesn't give the parent a chance to relax with, know, and trust the teacher or the opportunity to discuss in some detail what life is like for and with that child at home. Such information can be invaluable, providing the teacher with insights as to how best to befriend and motivate a certain child.

These parent conferences should occur either before school opens in the fall or during the first month of school. It's important to learn as soon as possible that Sam comes to school without breakfast after nights when his older brothers keep him awake until two or three in the morning. Or that Jill gets headaches in the afternoon and can't concentrate on her schoolwork.

Without this information, or if we don't get this information until four months into the school year, it's often too late to help the child. By this time, too, many teachers have already formed an opinion about a student, have decided based on what they have observed how capable a student is or that he or she is a "behavior problem." It's difficult to change these impressions once they're formed. Parents need the opportunity and time to inform a teacher or, in secondary school, a group of teachers and administrators.

Survey results also show that parents appreciate teachers who make themselves available for conferences outside the eight-to-four school day. Many parents, especially single parents, have to be at work during those times. They can't manage or afford to miss work to attend a fifteen-minute conference at school. Parents need some opportunities to meet in the evenings or early mornings with teachers. Of course, if teachers do make themselves available for parent meetings outside of the normal school day, the district should provide some type of compensation, perhaps a half-day for staff training or for personal work inside or outside of the building.

The irony is that school personnel strive to see themselves and want others to see them as "professionals" rather than as district "employees." We are the professionally trained experts in educating students in the schools. Our degrees and certifications state this. For as long as I've been teaching, teachers have recoiled against the eight-to-four mentality of signing into school and signing out, because they must put in so much extra time on evenings and weekends preparing to teach. As professionals, our role is to do the job well, not to do it on an hourly basis. Education is a business. We must, therefore, meet our clients when they can meet with us.

Parents want professionally trained, knowledgeable educators teaching their children. They want to know their children are with us, safe and learning, during certain hours of the day. However, when they meet with us they don't want our professionalism showing. Instead, they want the warmth and individual concern of the personal touch, often a difficult role for teachers to understand and fulfill.

WHAT DO PARENTS WANT FOR THEIR CHILDREN?

Either before meeting with parents or when meeting with parents, it helps to gather some specific information on paper, written by the parent or parents: What do parents want for their child in school and what do they expect from the school staff?

The following questions have been adapted from the "Goal Setting" form that Roosevelt Middle School teacher-advisers (they play a more proactive role than the traditional homeroom adviser in helping students) give to Roosevelt Middle School parents:

1. In what *three* classes or areas would you like to see your child improve this year?

2. What are the academic skills that you feel your child should focus on this year?

3. What other activities or opportunities would you like to see your child take advantage of in school this year?

4. Are there certain concerns, home situations, or medical problems, that the school staff should be aware of to work more positively and effectively with your child?

5. What ideas or suggestions might you give to help your child reach these goals?

A more general question sheet might provide additional parental input that could be used by the entire school staff throughout the year and might provide ideas for new programs for the following year. The following questions are adapted from the Roosevelt Middle School Curriculum Committee Parent Questionnaire.

1. If you had to choose the *three* most important things students need to know in order for them to become successful adults, what would these be?

2. How much input should parents have on designing courses for the school curriculum? How would parents provide this input?

3. How much input should students have in designing courses for the school curriculum?

4. What classes would you like to see offered that are not offered now?

5. In what ways can we best communicate student progress to 1) students and 2) parents?

6. What do you think are the *three* most important challenges students will face about their lives, community, and the world?

7. How can we help all students succeed?

8. Other comments:

Both of these questionnaires can produce a wealth of information to help individual students and to improve the school program as a whole. However, it's important that questionnaires like these two are not given to parents at the same time. They need to be spaced out so that parents don't feel overburdened. If parents do feel there's too much to answer, they'll either discard the questionnaires or answer very superficially. (Remember what it's like to go to your mailbox in school and find questionnaires from teachers, the principal, the district, the education organization. Mine "accidentally" get buried somewhere.)

To get an added benefit from these questionnaires, provide places for both the parent and student to sign. Students could read and discuss the parent's hopes, concerns, and ideas about their education and about school in general.

THE PARENT CONFERENCE

Parents have a right to be concerned about how well their children do in school, and how well the school works with and educates their children. In turn, the classroom teacher has to be allowed flexibility, a teaching style and choice of materials to best teach a wide variety of students. The best way to make certain both of these needs are met is to keep the communication lines open and informal and to be responsive.

I've found—as mentioned in chapter 7—that it helps a great deal to keep a folder or large annotated index card for each student. In the folder might be examples of the student's work and notes about the student's progress. The annotated index card, which I've used for over twenty years, lists individual assignments, test scores, and my general and specific comments on each assignment and on class participation and behavior, each item dated.

The typical grade book contains little specific information to convey to parents. The teacher has to try to remember—for that one student out of hundreds—what the specific circumstances were that led to a grade on a paper or test weeks or months before. If a student is not progressing well, a parent wants to know why, what's happening, and specifically, what the student can do to improve. Even if a student is doing well, a parent still would like to know how well and what their child has accomplished. How does the teacher know—besides looking at grades in a book—that a student is doing well?

Before the Meeting

Both the parent and teacher should understand the purpose of the parent-teacher conference. Is this conference just the routine, touching-bases meeting required periodically by the school administration? Is there a concern with the student's academic performance? Is there a serious problem with behavior, or behavior and academics? Should an administrator or counselor also be included in this meeting? Should the student be present? Should other teachers involved with the student be at the meeting?

If the meeting comes as a result of previous concerns and parental contacts, the teacher, ideally, noted each of these contacts: what the issue was, what was discussed, perceived attitudes, results, and date. These notes would be either in the folder or on the index card.

I've found that it helps to think through what you want to discuss with a parent before the meeting takes place. If this is the first time the parent has visited the school, or if you haven't met before, or if it is a meeting with a parent whose child has problems, gather some information and perceptions from others before the meeting. Has the student had problems with behavior? What were the circumstances? Which staff member handled the problem and what was the outcome? How does this child function academically and socially in different classes (seat-learning as well as activity-oriented classes)? What would others suggest to best deal with the student's situation and with the parents? Perhaps the counselor or nurse knows more about the student's background and family.

Just taking that little time to gather others' impressions and knowledge and being open to other opinions may affect your original perception. In turn, this may determine how you decide to manage the parent meeting and how helpful this meeting will be for the student and parent. Angry parents won't help a child succeed in school and certainly don't help the school itself.

If a parent sends a note or leaves a phone message requesting a meeting, it helps to call the parent and get some idea why the parent wants to meet with you. Sometimes, I've found there is just a simple misunderstanding; perhaps the child has given the parent a very one-sided account. In this case, I can often clear up the matter over the telephone.

If the parent does want a meeting with you, a phone call gives you some understanding of the issue involved and the parent's attitude. With this knowledge, you may then find additional information, support, and advice before the meeting takes place. It's very uncomfortable to be faced with a parent complaint when you don't have the necessary information to discuss the concern intelligently.

The Meeting

Ideally, the focus of the meeting will be on how parent and teacher can work together to help the student live a more happy, healthy, and successful life in and outside of school. Repeated accounts of what that student has done wrong, not done, or failed at doing, need to be mentioned and put aside as quickly as possible. There's only one direction to go: ahead, tomorrow, the future! How will things improve for this student?

I like to make the meeting as informal and personal as possible. When people sit near each other, it's much more difficult to become angry, or to not listen. So, I arrange desks in a little circle. If the student attends this meeting, I try to sit next to the student. This promotes the feeling that I like the student, want to help, want us to be friends. Sitting opposite the student tends to show a confrontational approach. Even if only one parent attends this meeting, I sit more to the side of or at an angle to the parent rather than directly opposite, so that we can share information and ideas.

No matter how serious the subject of the meeting, it helps if the teacher begins with something light—an anecdote, a humorous incident, a positive observation. The teacher wants people to relax, to release some of the tension and stress, and to focus on dealing with the concern, not personalities.

Because the parent should know what this meeting concerns and will, most likely, have information, ideas, and feelings to share, I like to focus on what the parent feels and sees as the main issue so that the parent feels empowered to express ideas and feels that the teacher is listening. In some cases, a brief opening statement about my concerns or staff concerns focuses the issue for all. Then, the parent might express an opinion or ask questions.

In any case, after the parent or student or other staff member makes a statement, the adviser-teacher should consistently paraphrase what that person said to see if all agree and understand. At times, it might be more appropriate and effective to ask the parent or student to paraphrase what has been said.

The next step deals with information sharing. Perhaps you review the student's folder or index card or notes from other staff members about this student. It helps if the tone of sharing can be maintained: "This is information we have, and some concerns expressed. How do you feel about these comments? Have you seen similar things happening at home or outside of school?" The next question would usually be, "Why do you feel things are happening this way for Matt?" At some point, offer your observations: "These are some of my concerns for Matt's success here."

If the student attends the meeting, and in most cases the student should—after all, it's the student's life being discussed—ask the student to comment on the problems: on why they've happened, on feelings about school, and on what others have said or observed. The student might even begin the meeting with these personal comments before the parent speaks to the group.

About half the meeting time might be spent on strategies, plans, and agreements to help Matt improve, succeed, and be happy with who he is and how he functions in school. The key here, of course, is that whatever the teacher or parent suggests must work toward positive outcomes, and both the teacher and parent must agree to follow through and support each other. If the student attends, then he or she should also agree to the suggestions or, at least, acknowledge awareness of them.

Try to leave a few moments at the end of the meeting to allow the student or parent to ask any questions and express concerns and feelings.

Take the time to write out the strategy with which you both or all agree—even if it's in an outline form. Date the agreement (all parties might initial it). Then, preferably before the parent leaves, photocopy the agreement for each person. This leads to fewer misunderstandings—and the teacher has a copy of the agreement in the student's folder.

THOSE DIFFICULT SITUATIONS

Sometimes a teacher encounters an angry parent or parents. The school—and, ideally, the district—should have an advertised policy or procedure for parents with concerns. If a parent immediately runs to the principal or the superintendent or the school board, the school people should refer the parent to the district policy and to the teacher contact. If the matter warrants a meeting, it should initially be between the parent and that teacher. A meeting that includes an administrator, the parent, and the teacher, not just the administrator and parent, is the next step. If this meeting does not resolve matters, then the administrator should help decide the next steps to be taken.

A formal school policy should especially apply to attempts at censoring materials, books, and what's being taught in a class. If a parent, or parents, object to materials, the teacher or principal should first ask that they read the material or book in total. After they have done this, the teacher might meet with the parents to discuss their concerns. It's important to have the parents specifically cite their concerns and explain why they object to the material. An administrator should be included in the conference. If matters cannot be resolved, the teacher might offer to substitute other readings for only those parents' children, without penalizing these children.

However, I feel that educators should not permit a few very vocal parents or adults to censor materials to which most students and parents do not have objections. These parents would then become dictators, determining according to their own religious, moral, or cultural beliefs what is taught and learned in school. They may have a right to do this for their own children, but not for other people's children.

Teachers, as professional educators, have the knowledge, skill, and judgment to choose appropriate materials. We need to stand up for the rights of the other students in our classes. We need to insist that administrators and school boards support us and not be cowed by a few raucous voices.

If a parent comes without an appointment or storms in angrily to a class, the teacher has the right to ask that parent to make an appointment so they can both calmly sit down and discuss the matter. This also gives the teacher time to review the situation and maintain control and focus of any meeting. The last thing a teacher wants to do is to try to talk with an enraged parent and then become angry also. Anger feeds on anger and escalates: Everyone loses.

When such confrontations take place, the first thing for the teacher to attempt to do is to "walk in the other person's shoes," see the situation from the parent's or child's point of view. Could their anger be justified? How so? If they do have some legitimate grounds for this anger and confrontation, the teacher should take a look at what might be done to rectify the situation, to make things better in the future.

The other step a teacher should immediately take is to create a folder of information (if this hasn't been done already) about the situation. This folder should contain the following information:

- How the situation occurred, including who was involved, dates, any witnesses if appropriate.

- What happened as a result of this occurrence. When? To whom? Who was involved in deciding the consequences?

- (This should be done for every call or meeting.) What parent contacts were made. When? What did the parent say? Attitude? What did you say? Your impressions of the exchange? Any decisions or outcomes?

- Names of any administrators, counselors, or teachers involved. In what way? When? What were the outcomes?

- Any additional student contact or behaviors after the incident. What? When? Who was involved? Outcomes? (The teacher should also note positive interactions to reflect a more balanced view.)

- Any notes, dated (and duplicated in case they must be shared) from parents, administrators, and students, including notes the teachers writes to others.

- If the conflict involves a student's work, copies of the student's work from the time of that assignment through the time the conflict is resolved.

- If materials used in class are challenged, copies of these materials or books along with other materials used in the same class to show relevancy or continuity. Were any class descriptions listing materials handed out at the beginning of the term?

Although any teacher desires the outcome to be as positive as possible and quickly resolved, it's important—especially in this day and with current attitudes—that the teacher take protective measures. We have all the responsibilities of being each child's "parent" while that child is with us at school and yet have little, if any, authority to act in the interest of the child.

Though a supportive, affirming letter from a parent may not be the usual, it certainly makes my day! The following letter concerns a student enrolled in my "Myths and Legends" class, an elective language arts class:

Dear Bob,

Peter has worked quite diligently on his project for your class and unfortunately he has not been able to finish for tomorrow. If you could allow him to present his material at his Friday class, it would be super. If this is against your modus, I will understand. I realize he has had three weeks to get it done.

My family does not go to church and your assignment brought home to me how little they know of the Bible. Although Peter had a couple of books for research, it was not enough. This past weekend I bought a book of Bible stories for children, and he and his sister have both been quite enthralled with it, and it's on Ben's required reading list for this year (by Mom). I want to thank you for bringing this great gap in their education to my attention.

WAYS TO HELP PARENTS WORK WITH THEIR KIDS

Most parents want to help their children, but they don't know how. They don't know what's expected and they don't understand today's curriculum. Their support, cooperation, and assistance are extremely valuable to the student and to teachers. Teachers, schools, and districts should find ways to help parents learn how best to help their children.

Parent Night

Nearly every school, I would expect, has a parent night when parents come to visit the teachers and classes at their children's school. I know, as a teacher, coming back to school in the evening and meeting all those parents can be wearing, but it means a great deal to the parents. (Usually those parents you most want to meet don't attend!) So let's try to reduce the stress on everyone and make the evening as informative and relaxed as possible.

Before parent night, each student should have made out a copy of his or her individual schedule of classes, the times, titles, and locations of those classes, and the teacher for each class. This can be handed to parents as they enter or as they assemble in designated places.

The night might begin with parents meeting in a homeroom or base room, where a teacher or administrator might explain the evening's schedule and intent. For example, we note that this is not a time for parents to discuss a child's progress in a class with the teacher. That should be handled with a scheduled appointment. Each parent receives a name tag to fill out and wear for the evening. We also ask parents to take a moment to provide us with any necessary information, and to drop off an evaluation of the evening with their comments before leaving. (These comments we post on the wall of the faculty room the following day, eliminating any negative personal references.)

Parents follow their children's schedules, spending about ten minutes in each class, with a five-minute passing time between classes and the scheduled break, and a time for coffee and cookies. During the ten minutes in class, the teacher could pass out a written description of the class, its intent, and expectations. Time should also be left for any parent questions about the class. It helps to keep the atmosphere relaxed. Some teachers begin with a funny anecdote, a joke, a brief game, a quiz, or an example of what the child does in that class. (We have a math teacher who dresses in various code colors or items: When he wears a certain tie, the students remember that there's a big test that day; certain socks might mean their assignments are due; a special shirt indicates a math game day in class. The kids love this! He demonstrates his "code dress" for parents, and they love it too!)

Parent Visiting Days

Parents have a right to visit their children's classes during the school day. They don't have a right, however, to disrupt classes with those visits. In general, our school has a policy of welcoming parent visits as long as parents give the teacher at least a twenty-four-hour notice.

Several times during the year, a school might have designated visiting days. Most high schools in Eugene have a Parent Swap Day: Parents attend the day's classes in place of or along with their children. (Few parents have the endurance to make it through the entire school day and wonder how their own children and the teachers do it.) Parents intending to visit should indicate this to the school several days in advance. The school should give each teacher a list of the parents who will be visiting which classes during that day. Of course, at the end of the visit, ask parents to leave their comments. (By and large, we have had very positive written parent comments. They prove very valuable to have on file—especially if someone challenges a certain school class or program or the way a teacher teaches. They also boost staff morale and commitment.)

Learning Nights

Several years ago, with the backing of the Eugene Education Association and the Eugene School District, I organized the first of our How to Help Your Child Learn nights. The basic concept was to assemble at a host high school a wide range of experts—teachers, counselors, and others—on education and children. Parents attended to learn and understand practical, constructive, and positive ways to work more effectively with their children. Each parent chose three sessions to visit during the evening. Some of the sessions offered included "Reading and Math for Kindergarten Readiness," "Skill-Building for Elementary School Readers," "Extra-Curricular Activities: When Is Too Much?," "Computers: Should My Child Have One?," "Improving Study Skills," "Your Teenager and the Law," and "Drug and Alcohol Abuse."

In later years, several of these sessions were organized into a more extended time frame. One evening each week over a twelve-week period, parents could attend a session focusing on one area and led by one or two experts. Such weekly meetings are a good way to get parents involved in the schools.

INFORMATION NETWORKS FOR PARENTS

Each month our school sends home a parent newsletter edited by our community-school person and filled with a wide range of information bits. For example, the newsletter lists important dates, events, and meetings affecting students and parents during the month. The principal writes a personal message about school, including thoughts on students, on students as children, and on the latest educational studies that relate to learning and children. Specific teachers or classes might share information about their unique activities or needs. Another section gives thanks to those parents who have volunteered in special ways, mentioning them by name. There's the "Help Wanted" list of school needs for parent volunteers and listings of community events for kids and families. Other topics might include "How To Stay Friends with Your Teenager," "Tutor News," "Learn a New Word a Day," "Homework—Too Much, Too Little—Help or Hindrance?" and the ever popular "Math Challenge" for parents—with a prize for the first to solve it.

Community-school coordinators have worked in almost every school in Eugene. They have proven to be a wonderful asset. Often, they organize and supervise after-school and evening activities in the school. The coordinators organize and supervise tutors, parent volunteers, training sessions, and visiting speakers. Most have developed their own resource banks of special people in the community for teacher use in classes.

I would expect that most communities and counties have community resource and information directories available for parents. However, few of those parents in need of various services even know they exist. Certainly, every school counselor should have one as reference, but so should every teacher in a school. When a teacher recognizes a need, that teacher can refer to this resource guide and respond to the need or parent immediately with helpful information. A typical parent resource guide contains the names of organizations for drug counseling, recreation, nutrition, working with teens, pregnancy support, medical/dental/psychological help, and more. If your community has not compiled one yet, please press to have such a guide published.

PARENTS AS VOLUNTEERS

Volunteers may be anyone from children and older students to senior citizens and may come from university, business, or neighborhood communities. However, the volunteers who have the most reason to participate are parents. Whether they help on a person-to-person basis, in class, in school, directly or indirectly, they benefit their children. So let's use parent volunteers more frequently and effectively.

As mentioned, a community-school coordinator may have already developed a volunteer resource bank that includes many parents and is, ideally, updated each year with the names of parents of new students. (Don't delete the parents of those children who have graduated: Often, because of the support and dedication of the school staff when their children were attending, they will gladly help out on a specific project.) If you don't have a resource bank, help organize one by using parent volunteers.

A sample volunteer resource questionnaire should begin with an opening statement to parents about the need for volunteers, the wide range of special ways parents might help, and their overall value to their children's education. Also, the school wants to reach out and try to involve those parents who feel they have little to offer, usually the parents of kids at risk. If we can help build the parents' self-esteem, then this may spill over to the child.

Areas covered on the questionnaire could include

- cultural background: Has the parent lived or visited in foreign countries or hosted foreign students? What are the parent's religious beliefs and customs and cultural background in terms of food, music, folklore, government, schools, art, history, and social customs?

- growing up: What were the parents' lives like as children and students, especially in different parts of the United States or of the world?

- working in the world: What do the parents do for a living? What are the rewards and frustrations of their work and what education is required? What happens to a paycheck?

- special talents, skills, interests: These might range from carpentry to stamp collecting, making masks, photography, cooking, music, and wilderness survival.

- helping in school: How would parents prefer to help? Provide suggestions: as an aide in the classroom, a paper grader, filing, in the office, or helping create and prepare materials to assist teaching.

- helping students: Suggestions might include tutoring; providing transportation, clothing, or food; serving as a "big brother or sister"; assisting a teacher.

A teacher could ask students to fill out the same questionnaire for their parents. The teacher might discover some parent talents even the parents didn't realize they had!

When a teacher asks for a parent volunteer, it's best to target the task. Few parents have the time today to commit to a full year or even several months of general volunteering. They tend to shy away from volunteering for large chunks of time during the year. It works better to ask a parent to volunteer for a special project or task for a specified period of time. In this way, each party—the parent and the teacher—knows what's involved in the parent's commitment.

It's extremely important to thank in writing those parents and others who volunteer, mentioning their names and what each contributed (not just the general "thanks a lot, parents"). In addition, the principal or staff member should write a personal note to that parent volunteer. (If a guest comes to my class to share, I write the thank-you note as well as give a note to the principal about who came and what that person contributed. It pays to do this. A quick thank-you to a volunteer at the door as students rush in and out doesn't mean as much and will not be remembered as long as a letter on school letterhead.

Toward the end of the year, as seems to occur in most schools that have volunteers, there should be an evening or early breakfast at school, maybe organized by the PTA or a similar parent group or the student government, to honor all the volunteers. Lots of praise, a certificate of thanks, a flower, or some food is a small token of gratitude for all that parent volunteers do for a school; but parents remember and will come to volunteer again.

PARENTS ON STEERING COMMITTEES

With the increasing interest in site-based funding, many schools in various parts of the country have included parents on the school steering committee. These parents actively participate in the decision-making process for that school. They help determine school philosophy and what will be taught, raise funds, assess needs, and problem solve along with the staff. Parents bring added insight and a wide range of abilities, plus they have a personal vested interest in seeing that the school program succeeds.

In any school, the following should be the case (from the "Weekly Staff Bulletin," Roosevelt Middle School, April 16, 1992):

1. Parents should feel that the school is friendly, helpful, and open to them.

2. Parents should be included as partners in helping their children succeed academically and socially in school.

3. Parents should be encouraged to comment on school policies, to offer suggestions, and, when possible, to share in decision-making.

4. School communication with parents should be frequent, clear, and two-way.

5. The school should encourage volunteer participation by parents and by the community at large.

REFERENCES

Armstrong, David. 1992. *Managing by Storying Around: A New Method of Leadership.* New York: Doubleday.

Gavzer, Bernard. 1992. "What Is a Family?" *Parade* (November 22): 14-17.

"Goal Setting." 1989. *Roosevelt Middle School Community Newsletter* (October).

Graff, Lisa. 1991. "Parents Deserve the Blame." *Eugene Register-Guard* (November 10): 1B.

Hunter, Madeline. 1989. "Join the 'Par-aide' in Education." *Educational Leadership* (October): 36-41.

Lindle, Jane C. 1989. "What Do Parents Want from Principals and Teachers?" *Educational Leadership* (October): 12-14.

Mitchell, Jann. 1992. "Redefining an Institution." *Oregonian* (June 22): 1C.

"Roosevelt Middle School Curriculum Committee Parent Questionnaire." 1992. Eugene, OR: Roosevelt Middle School.

Ryan, Michael. 1992. "How to Save Kids from TV." *Parade* (June 21): 10.

9

Staff Relations

The western mind has been programmed very narrowly: Define problems, seek solutions, set goals, make decisions, fix things. Fix your spouse, fix yourself, fix your children. When we see something we don't like, we judge it and want to change it rather than understand it: We look for the immediate solution rather than seek to understand why the problem arose.
—Dr. Jordan Paul and Dr. Margaret Paul
(Do I Have to Give Up Me to Be Loved by You?)

STAFF COHESIVENESS

It's important to remember that no two schools are exactly alike. From one year to the next, no school is exactly the same as it was the year before. Staffs, even the same staff from the previous year, change in terms of outlooks, attitudes, and relationships. Of course, the student population itself changes from one year to the next with the graduation of one-third of the students and the arrival of a new third.

The quality school remains flexible, open to change, and to realizing and meeting the needs of the new school year and new mix of students. The quality school relies on the core staff members to use their knowledge and experience to help the school focus on the shift in students' needs and lives.

We can help maintain and increase this flexibility through good interpersonal communication among all members of the school population. Staff members need to know each other to respond to needs and give support. A teacher who remains largely in the classroom cannot do this very well.

The consequences of isolation are lonely, unsatisfied teachers, lacking a shared technical culture of teaching and plagued by feelings of uncertainty about their ability to improve student learning. . . . Research suggests that successful schools, where student achievement is greatest, do not isolate teachers, but rather encourage collaborative planning and collegial relationships. (Johnston, Markle, and Arhar 1988, 28).

There are many teachers I like and respect a great deal, but I rarely visit with them because they happen to have a different lunch period than I do. It's difficult, except possibly at staff meetings, to know how these teachers feel and think about different issues and how well they as individuals are doing. For good staffs to work well together, there must be time to meet, to get to know each other, and to understand how each person feels and thinks.

An effective staff operates through consensus decision-making, not simply by majority rule. To gain consensus, members of the staff must understand and appreciate each other's fears and hopes, strengths and weakness, how each teacher thinks, and how each approaches working with students. To gain consensus, the staff must actively solicit and openly accept each staff member's imput.

The staff room becomes an important exchange place. Whether staff are eating lunch or spending part of a preparation period there, this room provides a neutral ground for getting to know others. Sometimes, a negative feeling develops toward those teachers who never or very seldom join others in the faculty room, creating the impression that they want to remain separate from the other staff members.

Preferably, the staff room atmosphere is informal. Some couches, soft chairs, and carpeting provide a more relaxing atmosphere. Pictures, cartoons, and quotes help too. It's nice to feel that in this particular room you can laugh a little more unrestrained, express ideas and feelings more openly, and feel some peace from the hustle of the school halls and day just beyond the staff room door.

Social staff functions are another important means for developing staff cohesiveness. "Fridays at 4" gatherings; teacher bowling leagues; potluck lunch meetings; and special events such as parties for holidays, retirements, and the beginning or end of the year provide opportunities for staff (including the secretaries, aides, cooks, and custodians) to get to know one another. Each school needs a social events committee to make certain these important staff gatherings occur regularly.

PERSONAL CONFLICTS

From time to time, personal conflicts arise in the school just as in any place of work. One teacher may say something critical of another; people may become angry over an issue; a student or parent may play one teacher against another. The key, like almost everything else in the school process, is communication. Teachers must keep communication lines open among themselves, must focus on the problem or the issue—not the person—and must deal with the problem as quickly as possible so that it does not become distorted. This requires some courage and determination. It means meeting with the other person involved and controlling hurt and anger.

The Master Teacher series (1989) of pamphlets recommends the following in dealing with issues involving another staff member:

- Don't waste your time becoming angry. The anger only fills you with negativity and may place you in a bad light with others who see your reaction.

- It is crucial that you go to the source of the problem or rumor to find out if your information is accurate. Most information we receive is secondhand and subject to biased interpretation.

- When you do meet with that person or persons, do so in a nonconfrontational manner. Perhaps that person is innocent, did say something that shouldn't have been said, or said it and it's become blown way out of proportion. The person may want to apologize or just resolve the matter but, if verbally attacked, may instead defend what happened and may even expand on the issue. So use a simple "I heard that . . . . Is it true?" Then allow the person to answer without interruption.

- After the person has stated what happened, you might calmly point out some of the results of what was said or done, how it affects you, what might have been a better way to handle the matter.

- Ask that person to help rectify the situation by means of an apology or some statement to the staff clarifying what happened and why. If the person doesn't know how to change what's happened, rather than let the matter fester, suggest you work together to come up with some plan of action to resolve the problem, or ask a third party to help.

- Can you trust and work with this person in the future? You will probably have to work together again because you are on the same staff and will likely have a good deal of contact with each other. It's very unpleasant to work with someone you don't like or trust, so, ideally, trust will be rebuilt. However, you also need to keep attuned to how that person relates to you and to indications that the same type of incident or behavior may occur again.

Field trips or special activities will cause students to miss classes. Avoid problems with other teachers by posting lists of students who will be absent and write a short explanation of the activity so that others understand. Do this at least a week in advance of the scheduled trip or activity and also make certain it's listed on the monthly activity calendar and that parents are notified. I get upset when a particular activity such as a performance by the storytelling troupe is scheduled and I discover the day before or that day that half of my class will be participating in some other activity. That's simply not fair or considerate—or good for staff relations.

SUBSTITUTE TEACHERS

I expect any teacher who substitutes for me to teach from my plans. I do not expect the sub to tell personal stories to each class, show films, or just do whatever he or she feels like doing. After all, the substitute teacher is a certified teacher. I have written notes praising those subs who followed through and given the principal notes on those who did not. If I have such expectations and my students know this, then the substitute teacher usually has an easier time. My students know, too, that the substitute teacher should be accorded the same respect and assistance as any guest in our building would receive.

One of my typical substitute teacher lesson plans might look like this:

Lesson Plan for Tuesday

The student index cards to record work ARE NEVER TO LEAVE THE ROOM AND ARE ALWAYS TO BE PLACED IN THE TOP DRAWER OF THE DESK. Students do NOT handle these cards.

No students are to be in the back room.

At your discretion, only one student may leave the room at any time—for a 3-minute period or so—to go to the restroom.

The attendance book is on the front desk.

Vicky, a student from the university, is here to help correct papers and record work, not to teach.

At the end of the day, please straighten the desk rows, and lock the windows and door. Lock the door whenever you leave the room.

1st/2nd Periods: "Treasure Connection" in Room B-7 with Alice.

We are working with interpersonal communication skills and family relations. Please help Alice.

3rd Period: "Movies and Writing" in D-4.

**** Make certain you have signed up for a VCR and TV before the school day begins. The video is in the bottom desk drawer. At the end of this period, rewind the film to where you began so it's ready for 7th period. Remove the video at the end of the period and return the VCR to the library.

Before the classes begin at 8:50, write the movie notes on the front board for the students to copy. These notes are attached to this lesson plan.

The movie this week is *Miracle Worker*, based on Helen Keller's life. Note the powerful emotions, frustrations, the determination of Ann Sullivan to break through the barrier of silence.

At the beginning of the period, read the board notes to the students and comment on them; allow them time to begin copying. Start the movie and leave a low light on for others to keep copying the notes.

Have Vicky collect and check off the *Josey Wales* papers.

THE ASSIGNMENT:

Using friendly letter form, each student will write ONE letter. This letter is to be from one of the characters in the movie. It is to contain at least three paragraphs:

- 1st par.: explains in detail who the student is in this film's story and how that character is involved in the story
- 2nd par.: explains in detail what that character sees as the main problem and presents examples of this problem
- 3rd par.: gives a thorough explanation of how this character would solve the problem, and the probable outcome of these actions

5th Period: The Troupe of Tellers.

This is a performing storytelling troupe. They are in two teams and operate independently. Teresa and Kelly will lead each team. Your main role is to supervise behavior and keep them on task.

I want the substitute teacher to be clear on procedures, on what each class is to accomplish, and to feel confident about following through on my lesson plan.

STAFF MEETINGS

I have yet to meet a teacher who looks forward to general staff meetings. Usually, the meeting is conducted by an administrator who has a specific agenda in mind. The meetings are long, boring, and tedious with few core issues openly discussed.

At Roosevelt, our teachers conduct these meetings (though admittedly some are still long and tedious). In some years, we have elected a chairperson for the year or for a term. In other years, a different teacher each month plans the agenda and leads. We have tried to restrict general staff meetings to no more than two a month, alternating between mornings before school and afternoons when school is over. (Of course, there are still the various subcommittee meetings, teaching-area meetings, and "emergency" meetings.) If the administrators do have matters to discuss with the staff, they put themselves on the agenda. For each agenda item, there is a suggested time allotment. If the staff wants to discuss the item for more than that time, then the staff must vote to extend for a specific number of minutes.

We've tried to focus at least one meeting a month on students. In the first part of the staff meeting, we share information—everything is to be kept confidential—about students who concern us because of academics, behaviors, or other personal problems. The counselor, an administrator, the house adviser for that student, and other teachers who have or had that student in class may share a photo, information, and impressions, positive and negative, about the student. Then we try to agree on specific strategies to help that student succeed. Each teacher who has the student in class may develop certain support strategies. However, even those teachers who do not have the student may look for the student in the hall and just smile and say hello or "How's your day going?" Even this small positive recognition can make a tremendous difference in the student's feeling of being accepted and acknowledged.

To make the students feel more a part of school, we have elected student representatives who join us at general staff meetings. These representatives may comment and vote, one vote each, on any matters brought before the group that concern or affect students. There have been several occasions when students voicing their points of view have swayed the staff's opinions, or when their votes have altered the consequences of some action. This validates their presence at the meetings. If they want to be on the meeting's agenda, they have that right. If they wish to sponsor a motion, they can do that too, as long as they've written the motion down and have three faculty members sign as sponsors to bring the idea before the general group.

Often a meeting begins with an activity to allow people to unwind, relax, and get their minds off the day's problems. Staff might take a few minutes to participate in a silly word game, play a twenty-questions game for candy bars, define what a "snerfoil" might be, or write the funniest nonsense sentence from a group of letters. In other instances, the first few minutes of a meeting might be given to listing our five "best hopes" and/or five "worst fears"—and sharing these in small groups. Teachers may be asked to write a short note of appreciation to some other teacher, the administrator, cook, custodian, aide, or secretary about a specific time that person helped or did an exceptional job. These notes create a sense of awareness and appreciation for what others do in school to help.

During the course of the meeting, if someone deems it appropriate, a motion may be made to discuss a particular item on the agenda. A vote is taken on the motion, which is passed based upon general consensus. General consensus, rather than a simple majority, helps show that there is commitment to following through on the motion. We need each person's willingness to follow through, or at least not impede the decision. Later, if necessary, we can reevaluate our action. If support is not forthcoming, then the staff has a right to know exactly why from any staff member who did not cooperate.

At a meeting, a staff member may comment that the behavior of another individual is helpful or not helpful to the issue under discussion. Individuals need to hear this said at times, but again, the focus is on the behavior, not on the person. Once a decision has been made, each member of the group owns that decision and is responsible for seeing it carried out. Confidentiality is important, too. Staff members should agree that issues and points of view, not a person, may be discussed and debated outside the meeting. At the end of each meeting, time is set aside for a debriefing to find out how people feel about what's been done and *how* decisions have been made. Staff members must feel safe to openly express their feelings without repercussions.

We find that we also need half-days or extended meeting times devoted to discussing major issues or problems arising at school. For example, behavior problems that occur in many classes call for more than just increasing suppressive measures. The staff needs time to look for the underlying causes of a pervasive behavior problem and time to brainstorm on creative, positive ways of dealing with the problem. The hour-long staff meeting is too short and too fractured to address such problems. Extended meetings are central to the overall philosophy and foundation of our educational program and goals.

Whatever is decided during the meeting, including pertinent pro and con comments on issues, should be kept in a staff meeting notebook for ready reference. Any staff person should be able to look in this notebook to see what happened, when, and why.

CHANGE

Teachers fear change. It's like starting over, losing the point of reference—the security blanket. Schools have remained basically unchanged during the past 150 years. Everything else in the world has evolved with amazing rapidity—transportation (will we return to the wagon?), communication (can we live with just typewriters?), productivity, family, and social structures. Schools, however, still remain largely in the factory mode because of politics and because both school staffs and the public fear change ("Let's go back to the basics!" "It was good enough for me when I went to school!") Yet, of course, schools must teach not for the present but for the future.

> Change is always threatening. When things change, people don't know where they stand. It's not surprising then that people invariably resist change.
>
> —David Armstrong
> *Managing by Storying Around*

The irony is that we expect our students to constantly change, to learn new things, and to risk themselves in learning, whereas we teachers don't want to do the same. We don't want to risk not knowing, admitting we're not experts, having to learn from others—including our own students—and, possibly, failing on that road to learning.

Perhaps the first thing we have to recognize is all the roadblocks we set up to stop change, to keep new ideas away. For example, we may sometimes

- overgeneralize with statements such as: "It always ...." and "You can never ....";
- have tunnel vision and make everything either right or wrong, allowing no room in between for modification;
- blame, accuse, and demand; and
- put others and their ideas down or use sarcasm.

We may even use set phrases to kill new ideas or any creative thinking:
- "A good idea, *but*. . . ."
- "It will never work!"
- "You don't understand."
- "Interesting idea, but we are different."
- "Too hard." "Too late." "Too early." "Too much."

David Armstrong came up with one good way to control negative response or feedback and "killer phrases." He gives each person at the meeting one M&M. If the person is about to or makes a negative comment, then the person must eat the M&M. If there is no M&M in front of the person, then that person cannot make a negative comment again during that meeting. He reported that his employees thought it was "great!" People didn't feel threatened by new ideas: They started to support them and think about them in positive terms. As he comments, "Minds are like parachutes: They only function when open" (1992, 136).

Change begins with brainstorming: If we could create the ideal school for students, what would we want to include and see happening? What would we like to see happening in terms of curriculum, atmosphere, technology, use of time, and how we teach and work together? There are no restrictions, no limits, no impossibilities! The focus is first on what we want for these particular students in this particular school and then on how we can get there.

Of course, Edward deBono's (1989) "six hats" approach, which we used to stimulate creative thinking with students, also works with adults. This method allows each person to express ideas and feelings without resorting to tunnel vision and killer phrases and encourages them to open up to new ideas and change.

The opposite of the killer phrases are words that welcome and stimulate creative thinking:

- "Great idea! Keep on with it!"
- "That's an interesting way to see it. I'd like to explore that."
- "I'm glad you brought that to our attention."
- "Go on . . . try it."
- "Fantastic!"

Notice the different feeling when you say these words versus the negative ones. There's an uplifting, an energy, an expectation and permission to try, go forth, explore—see what happens. Nothing is written in stone. Try the new idea! Just like a first draft of writing, the idea will probably need some revision, alteration, and rethinking. When that need arises, work with it, improve the idea together. We, ideally, teach our students this process—why can't we use it?

We must not focus on why things are impossible but believe they *are* possible and focus on how we can make them so.

Very seldom will an entire staff buy into some basic change in educational approach. Therefore, one of the best ways to begin change is to encourage some staff members to try a model program to see how it works, the concerns or problems, and adjustments that need to be made. Other members of the staff, however, must agree to make some adjustments in the schedule or change the way things have worked before to allow for this experiment.

Using this approach, two other teachers and I joined to team-teach a thematic class for a two-block period each day. This class, Reach Out, focused on helping students develop personal and interpersonal communication skills, self-confidence, and community participation.

Did we have a lot of adjustments, rethinking, coordination problems? Yes, we did! Three teachers truly trying to integrate curriculum and share equally in teaching proved to be a difficult goal to achieve. We did manage to teach the year-long class together in pretty good shape:

> It was my privilege to be a part of this class as a substitute teacher for three and a half weeks. I chose the word "privilege" carefully because I saw what should be seen by many: Middle school students opening up to one another with honesty about their lives in a setting of mutual respect and trust. True and sincere feelings came out from most of these children. . . . It is needed. It is appropriate. It should be expanded.
>
> (Letter from a substitute teacher, October 25, 1989)

The following year, after the three of us tried this approach, monitoring the concerns and results for the staff, five teams developed thematic classes with an integrated curriculum. This program has become a major ingredient of change in our school. Wonderful classes develop, such as classes examining different cultures through their art, the history of musical theater, archaeology, and traveling around the world—with various perils included—in 100 days. One class viewed the earth—its peoples and problems—from the point of view of aliens coming to earth! Exciting, interesting stuff!

Along with considering the flexibility people needed to develop and teach these classes, the staff also had to rethink how time is structured for the school day. Why forty-minute class periods? As noted, other countries don't employ such disjointed, hectic schedules. We combined two periods during the day for block classes of seventy minutes. To make the school day calmer in general for both students and teachers, we decided that classes in odd-numbered periods would meet, for seventy minutes each, only on Tuesdays and Thursdays. Classes in even-numbered periods (2, 4, 6, 8) would meet Wednesdays and Fridays. Mondays, each period would last thirty-five minutes. Monday would be the only hectic day in the week, something we hoped to change.

In a follow-up survey, 65 percent of the staff felt that this time schedule reduced stress for students and 90 percent felt that it improved the pace of the school day. Even more important, 68 percent of the staff felt that these thematic "connection classes" increased the sense of community and provided more of a focus on caring in the school. All agreed that with these classes, students were making better and more connections between different subjects and still had ample opportunity to develop writing, reading, speaking, and research skills. (Statistics from Roosevelt Middle School staff interview data, winter 1992.)

Change does not mean that what teachers have taught, or what the school program has instituted, necessarily has been off course or not beneficial for most students. It does mean that times constantly change and that schools must adjust to and be at the forefront of new expectations and directions. Change means simply that our students, who will be adults in a very different world than the one in which we were children, must be prepared to survive and work as productive, well-adjusted people in the twenty-first century. To help them, we must initiate change now and continually. But do take time to recognize what you've done so well all these years and to celebrate these accomplishments before you move forward on the learning-for-life road.

In order to facilitate change and make it as easy as possible for the students, the teachers, and others, teachers need continual support. Simply taking a workshop, listening to a speaker, or watching a video on, let's say, cooperative learning or team-teaching will not make a teacher into an instant expert or even make him or her feel competent in a new area. Teachers must be provided with ongoing training by experts in the field and with continuing support from those experts and other staff members and must have easy access to applicable materials. Experts must be able to provide assistance in constructive personal counseling, demonstrations, coteaching, and problem-solving when needed and requested. Teachers must be allowed to try and fail without feeling they are incompetent. In this way, change can occur and teachers can risk that change and can learn.

Dr. Jennifer James, in her book *Windows* (1987), notes traits that successful people have in common. These same traits could easily apply to successful school staffs. So we could say that successful schools and their staffs

- set goals for themselves and make plans;

- see these plans as being successful and worthwhile;

- work together to solve problems rather than become mired in blaming and negativity;

- realize they are in control and define the quality of life, the success, the atmosphere, in their schools; and

- understand that their joy, passion, energy, personal demeanor, and sense of humor form the foundation for student success as well as teaching success.

THE PRINCIPAL

As teachers, we should be well aware of the qualities we need in a principal in order to teach more effectively and to have a welcoming atmosphere that encourages students to learn.

A quality principal goes out of his or her way to establish a positive, informal atmosphere among the staff, including classified staff members and administration. The principal establishes this positive atmosphere

- through humor that doesn't belittle any person;

- through remaining accessible to staff members, students, parents, and other members of the community;

- by allowing people to express their ideas and feelings in safety;
- by sincerely listening to others' suggestions, opinions, objections;
- by dropping into the staff room just to chat and relax with teachers;
- by taking survey checks several times during the year on how staff members are feeling and why they feel that way;
- by communicating to all staff changes under consideration and the reasons for these long *before* any final decisions are made (there are no surprises); and
- by being as fair and evenhanded as possible toward all staff members, whether certified or classified.

In parent newsletters and staff bulletins, our principal often includes a note, sometimes an entire page, mentioning staff or student contributions:

"Hats off to Jane S. and Fred M. for their work in helping the *Romeo and Juliet* productions to be so successful!"

"Hats off to Cattie B. for doing such a fine job teaching the golf class and hauling all those clubs back and forth in her car for a whole term!"

"Hats off to Kate P. and Jill H. In a recent analysis of the biographical section in school libraries in our district, our library had the highest percentage of biographies about females."

The principal's recognition of contributions allows the rest of us to be aware of them and to gain appreciation for the extra things our staff members do.

Some bulletins guide us and help us focus in positive, nonthreatening ways. They might mention that

- we're all working hard and that most are doing their best.
- people are tired and stressed, and there doesn't seem to be enough time to get things done.
- we need to maintain the consistent program that we have followed all year.
- we must be sure to follow our agreements with each other.
- we need to keep a positive attitude, that we get what we expect and should expect students to continue to learn.

David Armstrong in *Managing by Storying Around* mentions that people know what their jobs are if the administrator has made the goals and objectives clear to them. "You have to earn the respect of the people you lead. They're not going to follow you just because a piece of paper tells them they're supposed to" (1992, 85). It's quite apparent that people who are happy and confident work harder.

> A quality principal has enough confidence in himself or herself and others to allow teachers to teach and students to learn. The principal's first commitment is to people, not to a building. The principal has the ability to share authority and to work with the staff for a quality education program.
> —Robert E. Rubinstein
> "A Teacher's View of the Quality Principal" (1990)

If at all possible, encourage each administrator to work directly with students. Ideally, each administrator teaches a class sometime during the school year. Administrators might even exchange duties with teachers for a class period. If this commitment is too much, then an administrator may agree to coteach a class for one term. Another alternative is for the administrator to become a house or homeroom adviser to a group of students for the year. At the very least, have administrators come to class to talk about what it's like to be a principal or vice-principal, how they feel about their jobs and the students they deal with, what their lives are like outside of school, and their interests.

Involving administrators in positive ways with students gives those administrators a different perspective, helps them understand what life is like inside the classroom (which they tend to forget quickly even if they themselves have taught), how the current times and conditions affect students, what students are thinking, and what teachers need to teach more effectively. Students also have a chance to see the administrators in a more positive, human light.

THE TEACHER-ADMINISTRATOR RELATIONSHIP

Some teachers try to "stay out of the administrator's way." They may look at the principal or vice-principal as an adversary, as a person who evaluates their job performances and as someone they can't relax with in a social situation.

Of course, such feelings affect a teacher's attitude and flexibility and increase stress levels.

The best way to work with an administrator is to take the initiative. Greet that person in the morning; stop for a moment to chat and be friendly. Stop at the office to say hello. Why not? People want to know they're liked and usually respond in kind. Even if you have questions or differences in opinion about issues or approaches, you must keep the doors of communication open. If not, the one who will probably lose the most, feel the most stress, and be affected in working is the teacher, not the administrator.

Preferably, the administration evaluates each teacher several times a year. Teachers should insist on this. I don't like being evaluated only once per year, because I am under pressure to perform the one time the administrator comes into my class. I can only hope the students cooperate! Being evaluated in this way is just as bad—with all the pressure, stress, and import—as taking a final exam! A visit like this has little to do with helping teachers improve.

I would much prefer the administrator drop in for informal visits to my class several times during the year, even if it's for only part of a period. After each visit, we can compare notes in a scheduled meeting. In such a meeting the teacher has the opportunity to chat about feelings and thoughts—in a nondefensive manner—concerning the class and to ask for the administrator's observations. Ask for suggestions on how you can improve, be more effective, or better relate to and help students. You impress the administrator with your concern for your students, your teaching, and your professionalism in soliciting positive, constructive feedback.

During the year, when I've scheduled a special event for a class, I ask the administrator (a written note is best), especially the one who will be evaluating me, to come in and observe. If it's appropriate and I can do so without disruption, I try to involve the administrator in the students' activity.

If some of the students have done some exceptional writing or carried out a very innovative project, I share the results with the principal—even take the work to the principal's office. If I receive a complimentary note from a parent, I copy and share this and how appreciative I am to receive such a note. It can't hurt.

Take the time, either orally or in writing, to thank the administrator for coming to class when you asked and for any advice or constructive feedback. Even if you don't like the advice and won't use it, the administrator did try in some way to help. Few teachers take the time to write notes of appreciation to administrators who do help and go out of their way to support teachers and students. You'd be surprised at how much a note like this means to an administrator who often spends much of the day dealing with discipline problems, negative parents, outraged community members, angry teachers, budgets, and other stressful matters.

If a problem does arise with an administrator, then the teacher needs to document every exchange—phone calls, notes, conferences, and room visits. It does not help you to say, "Well, I remember when you said or you did . . ." when you cannot specify the date and describe the occurrence with some detail. Just as with the parent encounter, every incident must be described:

- date, time, place;
- what happened;
- what was said by you and by the administrator;
- your feelings about the exchange and why you feel it might have occurred; and
- what happened as a result of this encounter.

The more details, the more objective and rational the account, the more credibility you have with your complaint or, if necessary, grievance.

Let's say there is an administrative policy or approach that you don't agree with or like, that you don't feel is good for the students or the school. Try to avoid running up to the administrator, cornering that person, and possibly getting into an embarrassing argument in front of others. In such a scene, the focus is on who's in charge, not on the issue.

First, solicit other staff members' points of view. These may clarify your position, give you added information, or help you decide against an actual meeting with an administrator. Just listen to others without pushing your own personal feelings about the matter, allowing others to speak freely.

If you still decide on meeting with an administrator to discuss the issue, write down the main points of your argument in a logical, progressive order. The focus should be on *why* this position or policy should be changed for the good of the students, teachers, or school. It helps greatly if you offer an alternative to the policy you want changed; objections in themselves do not solve the problem. The more rational and low-key your presentation, the more the administrator is likely to listen and to appreciate and consider your ideas. If other teachers attend the meeting also, all the better.

You have a great deal at stake in your relationships with the administrators in your school. Take the initiative to ensure that these relationships are positive.

(The school system is very "interesting": School administrators, central office administrators, and the superintendent supposedly function to support teachers and to see that students receive a quality education. These administrative people, who do not work directly with students in the classroom, largely dictate what the teachers must and must not do. Teachers are evaluated each year by these administrators, but rarely do the teachers have the opportunity or right to evaluate how well these administrators *do* support teachers and students. Why do we allow this?)

In May 1993, our principal of four years, a very innovative administrator committed to quality education for kids, left our school to become principal of a school in England. The following is the letter he sent home to parents.

Dear Parents:

This is my last Roosevelt newsletter. I have been at Roosevelt four years now. . . . As I leave, I want to share a few thoughts with you.

First, I would like to thank you for providing me with a tremendous amount of support, concern, and care. You mean a great deal to me. By working together in such a positive manner, we have helped to create one of the finest schools in the country. It is only through working together that we have achieved this success for the children in this community that we have. As you have done with me, I encourage you to continue to question and work with whomever the new principal is to help make things even better for Roosevelt kids.

I would also like to thank our Roosevelt students for being the outstanding students that they are. The reason I care so much about education is due, in large part, from working with Roosevelt kids and observing their outstanding accomplishments. Students from Roosevelt are terrific. I will miss them greatly.

Lastly, I would like to thank the Roosevelt staff who, in my mind, exemplify what a school staff should be: people of love, courage, humor, and a peculiar kind of wisdom that celebrates children and helps them to learn in the best sense of that word.

My wish for each of you is that you will continue to work to celebrate and be advocates for the well being of the children in our society. I continue to believe that the well being of children is not accorded a high enough place in our thoughts. That troubles me, and it should trouble you. We need to remember that our children are the messages we send to a time we will not see. They are the future! We need to do everything we can to advocate for children in a society that sometimes has too little regard for its children and its schools. We need to honor the best that our children are and help to make them the best that they can be. I believe that our future can be a better one by all of us working together in this kind of child advocate role. . . . Keep being positive and working together.

Sincerely,
Jim Slemp, Principal
Roosevelt Middle School
May 1993

REFERENCES

Armstrong, David. 1992. *Managing by Storying Around: A New Method of Leadership*. New York: Doubleday.

deBono, Edward. 1989. "Creative and Lateral Thinking" workshop. Portland, OR, December 8.

James, Jennifer. 1987. *Windows*. New York: New Market Press.

Johnston, J. Howard, Glenn C. Markle, and Joanne M. Arhar. 1988. "Cooperation, Collaboration, and the Professional Development of Teachers." *Middle School Journal* (May): 28.

Paul, Jordan, and Margaret Paul. 1983. *Do I Have to Give Up Me to Be Loved by You?* Minneapolis, MN: Compcare Publications.

Rubinstein, Robert E. 1990. "A Teacher's View of the Quality Principal." *Educational Horizons* (Spring): 151-52.

Slemp, Jim. 1993. "From the Principal." *Roosevelt Middle School Community Newsletter* (May): 2.

"When a Colleague Is Shooting You Down." 1989. Master Teacher (series) (February 13).

10

Dealing with Job Stress

Your ultimate goal should be to live in harmony with all aspects of yourself.

—Dr. Dennis T. Jaffe
Healing from Within

LAUGHTER

Laughter—enjoying the bizarre, the silly, the fun side of teaching and kids and being in school—has helped me over the past twenty-three years to survive the stress of teaching middle school with all the accompanying chaos and young hormones. I love to recount the time about fifteen years ago when I taught my Monsters class and asked each student to create an original monster in a story. One very sweet, innocent, seventh-grade girl created an octopus monster. In her description, she accidentally substituted the word *testicles* for *tentacles* and, as a result, added a peculiar twist to her monster tale.

We need to laugh more at work and about what happens with our work. Laughter eases tension, relaxes muscles, opens the mind, and allows us to see the world from a different perspective.

I like to collect what I call "slips-of-the-pen" that I find when evaluating students' written work. I love to discover creativity, original thinking, and progress in the students' work, but I dread evaluating all those papers! I calculated that I must read and evaluate roughly between 2,500 and 3,000 pages of student writing each year! Mind-boggling!! So collecting these "slips-of-the-pen" provides one way to help make evaluating all these pages a little more fun.

Here are some I enjoyed:

"The old lady fainted. So they called up the emergency people, who put her on a stretcher and carried her out through the revolving door."

"As for her physical detail, she's about 5'2" with glossy black hair, and breasts the size of Brazil!" (I had asked them to focus on physical detail. He did!)

"On top of this, my mother weighed 450 pounds, so I couldn't just snuggle up to her anytime I wanted. I had to be very careful!"

Take a moment to remember or jot down some of the funny things that have happened during your teaching career and in your life in general.

An *Industry Week* article about humor quotes from Charles Metcalf and Roma Felible's book *Lighten Up: Survival Skills for People Under Pressure*:

> The truth is that humor in the work environment (in combination with management's guidance and support and having the freedom to explore ideas) leads employees to become better, more creative problem solvers. . . . Employers ought to be begging to help people find the most enjoyable, fulfilling and creative ways to do their jobs. (l992, 18)

Metcalf and Felible also note that workaholics, although they put in many more hours on the job, rarely accomplish more than people who are less driven and have learned to relax. According to a Northwestern National Life Insurance survey, one-third of today's workers say that the stress they feel about their jobs will lead to job burnout. Twice as many workers as in 1986—some 46 percent—feel their jobs are highly stressful. Steps must be taken to reduce the stress.

Humor is one way. Metcalf and Felible note that we need to

- step back and see the absurd side of different situations,

- recognize that we must take ourselves lightly and our work seriously, and

- realize that life should be joyful. (1992, 22)

Humor may take the form of crazy messages between staff members, little pranks, silly sayings or cartoons posted on walls or put in mailboxes, or outlandish dress-up days. (Think of how kids might feel about school if they saw their teachers enjoying themselves and having some fun at school.) Many of the teachers at Roosevelt, along with the kids, dress up in costumes on special days. Our resident cowboy-physical education teacher made a wooden frame for "Cowboy Sayings" and hung it in the staffroom. Each week he brought in new words of wisdom from cowboy philosophy. They were great!

> The kind of humor that seems most stress releasing is the kind where we are capable of laughing at ourselves. We make fun of our own traits, laugh at our habits, or joke about our weaknesses. . . . Seeing the humor in our difficulties or in our pain requires distancing. This emotional distancing alone can obviously be of help in lowering our level of stress. (Greenberg 1980, 128-29)

What would happen if we could convey this sense of laughter and fun to our students? Possibly, we could create a "humor corner" in our classrooms—as well as in the staffroom—and suggest to students who feel depressed, discouraged, or angry that they spend some minutes during class or at other times in that humor corner reading what's there.

EXERCISE

Standing in a classroom and walking down halls is not the exercise one needs to relax muscles, reduce tension, and feel loose and easy.

I know that I need to exercise regularly, every morning, or I will not feel good during the school day, and that shows in my teaching and work with kids. Every morning I do stretching exercises for fifteen to twenty minutes before breakfast. Three mornings a week, by 6:30, because I know I have too many errands to do after school, I am at the spa for an hour of swimming, hot tub, steam room, and sauna. Then I go off to school relaxed. At night before going to sleep, I do a few minutes of stretching exercises. Lately, I'm trying some tai chi.

Sometimes, I take a half-hour or an hour walk in the early morning or at night. According to Dr. Gayelord Hauser (1974), walking helps cure a wide range of ailments such as tension, insomnia, and constant fatigue and aids digestion and circulation (151). The short amount of time you may use walking vigorously—maybe in the gym or outside during preparation time or lunchtime in the school day—helps you refocus and concentrate after the walk.

During the school day, take a few moments to stretch, especially when you feel tense and feelings begin to build: Stretch your arms and shake them out; do the same with your legs. Slowly rotate your neck first in one direction and then in the opposite. Stretch and flex your fingers, wrists, toes, and feet. Rotate your back from side to side. You might do these exercises for a few minutes between periods or while students are working quietly. It is best to do them *before* you get tense.

You might begin a class by taking a few minutes to lead the students in stretching and loosening-up exercises, tai chi, or improvisational drama exercises. This would give them—and you—some moments to relax and shake out the tension and a chance to refocus on the upcoming class. (This works especially well before students must take major tests, give presentations, or sit for long periods of time.) During this stretching time, you might review course material by throwing out questions and having the class answer in choral response. No student is put on the spot, and those students who don't know the answers hear them from other students.

When you are under stress, according to Dr. Herbert Greenberg (1980) in his book *Coping with Job Stress*, your heart beats more intensely, blood pressure rises, respiration increases, and there's a release of blood fat and serum cholesterol into the body's system (63). Dr. Greenberg noted that stress "is required for activity, productivity, and survival. But this is a good stress situation" (44).

In "bad stress" situations, we must take steps to alleviate the tension or suffer the consequences. Obviously, with such bodily reactions taking place, this is no time to sit, to try to sleep, or to be inactive watching television. Taking pills, drinking coffee or liquor, and smoking do not do away with the stress but only mask it for a brief time. Exercise is the best way to utilize those bodily changes and channel them into more positive and productive paths.

SELF-AWARENESS

Dr. Dennis Jaffe (1980) observes that when we are asked to be sensitive to what's in the room we're in, we may describe any variety of items and conditions. The one item people constantly overlook, however, is themselves.

How do you feel? What is your breathing like? Are your muscles tense or relaxed? Does your mind feel fresh and active, or tired and confused? When do you work well in this room and when not? Is there some type of pattern? If so, why?

Do you feel angry a lot? Anger, Greenberg notes, is one way to cover up feelings that are too painful or difficult to face. Anger rarely accomplishes anything positive or productive. If directed at another, it becomes destructive. If the other person becomes angry, then the anger is likely to escalate—maybe into physical and verbal violence. We need time to separate ourselves from those angry feelings.

> You can't burn out, if you've never been lit!
> —Stephen Glenn

Even without such anger, we all need quiet time, a time to sit and focus on ourselves. When the school day is over and the kids leave, I want to escape from the building as quickly as I can. Some teachers can stay and work for several hours; I cannot. I know I'll spend time at night and on weekends evaluating papers and preparing materials, but by 3:30 or so, I need a break from school and from people. I am mentally and emotionally wiped out!

Sometimes I just run errands, go for a walk, or look at stores. Other times, I go home to my study where, if my son is not blasting the stereo overhead, I can have some quiet time to myself.

So find a space or a room. Sit there with your back supported and eyes closed. Do some deep breathing and concentrate on different parts of your body. How does each feel?

Here some healing visualizations may be useful. Does a part of your body hurt or bother you? If so, concentrate on that specific part and its problem. See it in your mind. Then visualize, pour your mind's energy into seeing that body part as healthy and functioning well. Often, with repeated efforts and good concentration, your body will feel better.

In much the same way, during this quiet time, you can choose to visualize and focus on a specific problem or concern you have in school. See the problem or scene in your mind. Then picture the problem being resolved in a positive way. Perhaps, through this visualization, you will find the will to take an action that resolves the conflict. Many sports figures and performers have effectively used visualization to reduce stress, resolve conflicts, and improve their own effectiveness. Why not teachers?

Could we help students by teaching them some of these techniques? What if students—all students—visualized themselves as successful, as learning, as enjoying school?

WE ARE WHAT WE EAT—UNFORTUNATELY!

I no longer eat red meat and eat many more salads and vegetable dishes. I think this has helped my digestion a little and has cleared up some of my stomach problems. But I will not give up chocolate! That's too much to ask!

Dr. Hauser states that reducing stress is definitely related to changing our diets: "There's more evidence that the fountain of youth is good nutrition—fresh, unprocessed food, exercise, relaxation, a zest for life. . . . I believe a well-fed body is the best defense against the tensions of modern living" (1974, 7).

Dr. Hauser warns against consuming large amounts of dairy products because many people find they're allergic. He recommends "good" protein, whole grain cereals, salads, snacks of cheese, whole wheat crackers, nuts, peanut butter, orange juice, skim milk, and honey as some healthy diet components.

Drinking only coffee for breakfast lowers the blood sugar dramatically. Consuming greasy, heavy fast foods causes tiredness. If you have low blood sugar, you may feel tired and weak, have headaches, and feel dizzy and unsteady. "We certainly see hypoglycemia (low blood sugar) in sugar addicts, in alcoholics, in coffee and soda addicts. People who have studied hard-drug addicts report to me that hypoglycemia is common among them" (Hauser 1974, 14).

I find that an hour after I have lunch, I have difficulty staying awake, sometimes having to press my back against the metal window edge to keep alert and pay attention to the students. I've been told by a doctor that I probably have hypoglycemia. Part of the problem is going for long periods of time without food. Small morning and afternoon snacks help. I try to have some peanuts or protein crackers to snack on, but often I forget to eat them or become too busy. I'm still trying to find a solution to this condition.

THE COMPUTER EFFECT

Both students and teachers spend more and more time working with computer video display terminals in school and at home. The computer often proves to be a wonderful aid in learning. However, using it over long periods of time produces stress and health problems that teachers should note because these problems may affect both them and their students.

Computer use can produce neck strain, eye weariness and strain, headaches, blurring vision, and itching or burning eyes. People wearing bifocals can also experience problems because the video screen is too close for distance lenses and too far away for normal reading.

My optometrist concluded, after my recent vision examination, that I should use "computer glasses" when I work with a video monitor. They now make special glasses just to work with computer screens!

Teachers may be able to minimize the effects video screens have on students. Glare on the screen can be reduced by wearing dark-colored clothing and adjusting window blinds. Sometimes, rooms are overlit for computer work. Removing some bulbs and maintaining a cool white light improves conditions. Suggest that students try to blink more if their eyes burn and that they take "eye breaks" by looking at other objects at varying distances for a few moments or by standing , stretching, and walking around.

SELF-DEFENSE

I teach sixth- through eighth-grade students in middle school. The size and weight variations among students is immense!

One year, we had a student who stood about 6' 4" and must have weighed well over 200 pounds. In addition, this student had emotional problems, violent outbursts and had been suspended several times from school for violence against other students. Teachers felt intimidated by him and were concerned about their own safety. I'm medium height and build. Although this student and I got along well in class and I had no particular behavior problems with him, I sometimes wondered what I would do if he did become violent.

We find in today's secondary schools that more and more students are growing more quickly. They now are frequently stronger and bigger than their teachers. We also find that due to today's family situations—crack babies, emotionally damaged children—we have to be concerned about student safety and our own physical safety.

I have taken, and recommend that every secondary school staff person take, a one-term personal self-defense class. The National Education Association has noted that over 900 teachers are threatened with bodily harm every day in this country and that 40 of them are actually assaulted each day. Perhaps the school district, especially in inner-city areas, should provide such a class.

A well taught self-defense class doesn't promote the use of violence but rather gives you insight into ways to control violent behavior to varying degrees. This course provides you with the ability to assess situations, defend yourself, and if necessary, safely disable an attacker. In effect, it builds your self-confidence and makes you feel less intimidated or vulnerable.

RELAXATION

Aristotle said, "The end of labor is to gain leisure." With this in mind, "leisure" equaling relaxation, we should try to focus on those behaviors that will bring us to a relaxed state.

Evaluate classroom activities. What's really necessary for learning? Eliminate what isn't. How might both you and your students participate in necessary activities in a more relaxed and easy manner?

We should take a look at our mind-sets. Speaking in positive terms promotes positive feelings. Remember the old adage: The glass is half-full, not half-empty. Look at what the students have learned and accomplished, not at what they haven't learned.

We must try to get away from school and school life more. (Several teachers I know seem to feel that they have to choose between being devoted teachers and having families. Teaching is very intense for them and consumes much of their energy. They spend so much of their personal time outside of school with students that they feel they cannot be both effective, caring teachers and effective, caring parents. They have chosen not to have their own kids.) Take time for yourself. Learn to gauge your energy so you can spend some quality time with friends and family. Try waking up fifteen or twenty minutes earlier than usual. Not having to rush, maybe having a few quiet moments to yourself in the early morning, gets the day off to a less stressful start.

I like to make lists of what I want to do each day in school, after school, and of people I need to contact. This keeps me focused. I don't have to spend time and feel the anxiety of trying to remember. I usually accomplish most of what is on the list. And I can see what I've done, rather than worry about what I've forgotten to do.

If I have appointments or must go to a place where I may have to spend time waiting, I bring along papers to evaluate or a book to read. Then my waiting time becomes productive time.

I don't make lesson plans per se. I do, however, list what I want to accomplish over a period of time with a certain class, or with a specific student, and how I'm planning to get there. This gives me a sense of direction as well as the flexibility to innovate. I don't usually have the anxiety of "what should I teach today?"

It's been difficult for me, but since my cervical disk operation, I've learned to say no more to others who want me to be on this or that committee, perform for free, or whatever else. You have just so much time and energy. Learn to say no sometimes.

Every day take the time to do something that you really want to do and enjoy doing. This may be a very little something—perhaps eating a good piece of chocolate!

Take a moment to list what kinds of pressures and tensions you feel in your life now. Who are the most important people in your life? What are your most enjoyable and important activities? What changes can you make in your life that will allow you to spend more time with these people and have a chance to enjoy some of these activities?

Set realistic goals for yourself, for your students, and for your family. Remember that the most important part of any goal is the journey of small accomplishments to attain it, not necessarily the goal itself. So, take joy in those smaller steps accomplished along the way.

REFERENCES

American Optometric Association. 1991. "VDT User's Guide to Better Vision." St. Louis.

Dewey, Jack. 1986. *Burned Out!* Shelburne, VT: New England Press.

Family Vision Center. "Focusing on Computers with over 40 Eyes." 1991. Eugene, OR.

Greenberg, Herbert M. 1980. *Coping with Job Stress.* Englewood Cliffs, NJ: Prentice Hall.

Hauser, Gayelord. 1974. *New Treasury of Secrets.* New York: Farrar, Straus & Giroux.

"Humor: An Antidote for Terminal Professionalism." 1992. *Industry Week* (July 20): 15-18.

Jaffe, Dennis T. 1980. *Healing from Within.* New York: Alfred A. Knopf.

Klarreich, Samuel H. 1988. *The Stress Solution.* Toronto: Key Porter Books.

Metcalf, C. W., and Roma Felible. 1992. *Lighten Up: Survival Skills for People Under Pressure.* Reading, MA: Addison-Wesley.

11

We Are Public Relations!

A hundred years from now it will not matter
what my bank account was,
the sort of house I lived in,
or the kind of clothes I wore.
But the world may be different because
I was important in the life of a child.
                                                    —Anonymous

If we want to teach well, then we must communicate effectively—in clear, positive, exciting ways. If we want public support for schools, then we must also communicate effectively—in clear, positive, exciting ways and through as many different channels as possible. We must challenge public misconceptions about schools and make certain the public hears the facts and both sides of school issues.

Teachers are the public relations people for the schools, and our students carry the messages. However, we must go beyond relying on the students to communicate what we're doing in school, our successes and failures, our hopes and frustrations. Karen Famous, president of the Oregon Education Association, wrote,

> It has been said that over 90% of communication is perception. As education employees, we know that the public perception of education is certainly different from what we know to be true. . . . We should think of ourselves as public relations people for education—no matter what our positions are in the education system. . . . We need to advertise our successes. (1989, 8)

When we look at how our society depicts schools, we should cringe—and realize that we must actively work to correct these perceptions. For these perceptions affect our students' attitudes and willingness to learn and to succeed as well as our own effectiveness as teachers, the resources available to our schools, and the future of public education.

Notice how much attention star athletes receive in our newspapers and in our schools themselves, sometimes most of a page in the city's paper. Then note how much attention and value is given to the student who wins a science award, gets a scholarship, or edits the school newspaper for an entire year. We can make the local papers aware of such discrepancies through phone calls to editors and letters to the editor, suggesting that they focus on other than just athletic accomplishments.

The late summer and fall ads often refer over and over to the doom and gloom of returning to school. Students should buy these shoes, clothes, and bikes, to counteract the impending horror. Advertising near vacation time focuses on the chance to escape from the "prison" of school. This is a fine way to impress on our children the importance of education! But we can phone or write these advertisers and merchandisers and tell them we don't appreciate the negative tone of their ads about education and school. We can have our teacher organizations, from the local to national level, publish articles and write letters protesting this negative characterization of schools. Don't forget to also take a moment to write and give support to these groups when they create ads or write articles that reflect positively on education and learning.

Add to all of this the portrayal of teachers and schools on television. Teachers are depicted most often as weak, selfish, difficult, inefficient, problem-ridden people in a chaotic, angry atmosphere. We then have a self-fulfilling prophecy, a model for our young people watching these television shows, buying advertised products, and attending school with these instilled expectations. We need to speak out and write letters about these shows.

When antieducation politicians like those in the Reagan and Bush administrations politicize and purposefully distort education and school problems, we cannot just stand by and shake our heads. According to Harold Hodgkinson, director of the Center for Demographic Policy, Institute for Educational Leadership,

> The Reagan Administration and the Bush Administration complained that we are throwing money away on education. However, the data they cite to show Americans spend more than any other industrialized nation on education includes the figures for higher education, on which we spend a prodigious amount. (The U.S. has 5% of the world's elementary and secondary students and 25% of the world's higher education students.) (1991, 14)

And *Education Week* published:

> According to their January 1990 report, The Economic Policy Institute ranks the U.S. 14 out of 16 industrialized nations in school spending at the precollegiate level. To bring precollegiate spending up to the average level in the other 15 countries, the U.S. would have to raise spending by $20 billion a year. (January 14, 1990, 15)

We should vociferously ask why the U.S. Congress spends more on itself—approximately $2.8 billion in 1992, for example—than any other legislature in the world. Why have congressional salaries risen to $129,000 a year, an amount that ranks within the top 2 percent of American salaries, and why have their staffs of paid aides quadrupled to 20,000 people? We should demand more of an accounting for the nearly $2 trillion that congressional members control in spending and loan guarantees annually ("Taxpayers," 1992, 9). Tom Clyde in a *Newsweek* article asks, "Why is there no money for textbooks but $20 million to pave a little Utah dirt road that affects 600 people?" (1992, 11).

Reading about abuses like this when I'm teaching thirty-plus students per class in a building that needs repairs and with a lack of books or desks or up-to-date education materials and equipment for my students makes me furious! I would hope you feel the same—and that we both shout about these frustrations and demand change.

THOSE STUDIES ON EDUCATION

The number of "national" (any group can call itself national) education studies seems to multiply each year. They come to some very righteous, often politically motivated conclusions about what reforms are needed in education. Seldom, however, do they consider how these reforms can be realistically implemented. Teachers and schools continue to "fail" because they do not or cannot implement such reforms, mainly because of lack of funds, lack of support services and training, and lack of time to learn and use such new approaches.

When we look at who composes most of these "major" educational studies, we find committees that most often include political figures, "prestigious" people, college administrators, education professors, business people, and superintendents of schools. In general, these people have little first-hand knowledge about what it is like to teach daily in today's public school classrooms.

Seldom are classroom teachers on these committees. Yet we know that classroom teachers are professionals who have devoted their lives to teaching children. The teachers determine what will, what can, and what won't work in the classroom. We should point out that politically slanted, so-called thorough national studies such as *A Nation at Risk* (1983) are prepared by such committees. We should insist that teachers constitute from 20 to 40 percent of these committees.

Former President Bush's slanted *America 2000* (1991) report emphasizes school choice, voucher systems, subsidized payments, and tax breaks. All these proposals favor the rich and the white educational elite. Such reforms would gut the public schools and leave minorities, the disabled, and children at risk—those with educational or emotional problems—in a much worse state. Who protests this?

America 2000 neglects the role of teachers as agents of change in the classroom and includes little mention of assistance to teachers who want to improve their skills. Larry Linkin, a noted music educator, in evaluation of *America 2000* stated that

> nowhere are music and the other arts mentioned, even in passing. . . . In other words, music and the other arts, unlike the so called "Five Basics," are, in the view of "America 2000," nothing more than the avocation of a few noisy parents and a gaggle of lobbyists with an axe to grind. . . . Music and the love of it will no longer be a cultural treasure, but more and more a privilege, tied to personal, family and class economics. (1992, 3)

When it comes to district budget cuts, the arts are cut first as a frill, as extras not needed. Those making the cuts don't seem to understand the impact that the arts or sports often have on young people. The arts and sports provide the meaningful connection—enjoyment and success—for the at-risk student, for the student who has nothing at home. The arts provide the main source for student expression, creativity, originality, inventiveness—all of which we need to stimulate our economy and keep us a great nation. "The ancient Greeks understood that the arts were not window dressing but the foundation, not just style but actual substance. In classical education, you didn't study any discipline until you mastered the arts. They understood intuitively what we now know and can document scientifically" (Keefer 1992, 1D).

Of even more concern is the fact that this *America 2000* plan did not take any notice of such educational issues as poverty, equal education opportunities in the public schools and between states, or school funding. These issues remain critical to any efforts concerning educational reform. Why haven't teachers and teacher organizations acted more strongly to point these things out?

It will be a great day when the schools and arts have all the money they want, . . . and the armed forces must hold bake sales to get the money for a new bomber.

—Anonymous

As educators, we must also stand together against censorship. If we take a close look at organizations that support censorship and the reasons they want certain books or subjects banned, we find that very often banning these pushes their specific points of view onto the general school population. Frequently, too, such as with their attempts to ban *The Diary of Anne Frank*, the group's underlying agenda is racial, religious, or ethnic prejudice. Several years ago, when I protested the removal of a good, young adult novel from our junior high library because of the efforts of two vociferous parents, who had never read the book, a downtown administrator told me to "mind my own business." I insisted it was my business.

THE NEED TO INFORM THE PUBLIC

In most communities in the United States today, 60 to 70 percent of the people may *not* have any children in schools and have little contact with schools other than what they read in the newspaper or see on television. As Walter Hoadley points out,

> The media have little or no interest in helping to find positive public consensus. News emphasis is continually on the discomfort levels of individuals and less than perfect performance in a world of human imperfection. . . . The need now is for greater understanding of what's really going on and the personal stake each of us has to help improve the outlook. . . . Far more is going right in America than wrong, certainly compared to the rest of the world. (1992, 39-40)

The public needs to know more about our schools.

- The percentage of high school graduates rose from 10 percent in 1910 to 84 percent in 1992.

- The National Assessment of Educational Progress (NAEP) test scores have remained remarkably stable over the past twenty years.

- There is a definite correlation between a child doing his homework and a parent at home to supervise.

- *Scientific American* did a study on Asian refugee children and why they succeeded so well in school. Their study showed that the crisis in our schools is far more social than academic.

- Over the past twenty years, the percentage of our GNP spent on our schools actually *fell* from 4.2 percent to 3.6 percent, despite the effects of inflation.

Again, we must actively and effectively utilize our communication skills to convey these points to all people in the community.

In most communities, school budgets are routinely defeated so that no new or higher taxes will be imposed. This generation, unlike past generations, has little commitment or willingness to invest in the future of our society through education or children. "What scares me about the processes of community budget decisions is the questions are framed in terms of, 'We don't have enough money,' and, 'What do we want?' Rather than, 'What kind of life do you want to lead?' " (Neill Archer Roan, quoted in Keefer 1992, 1D).

The public thinks it's saving money by voting down taxes for schools and refusing funding for school programs. The public will, though, vote to spend more money to build prisons and to hire more prison guards and police. As

Harold Hodgkinson (1992) notes, we need to make the public aware of the following:

- The get-tough policies now being implemented as a way to deal with drug-related crime will likely boost the U.S. prison population to over 2 million by the year 2000.

- The cost of maintaining our prisons, not to mention building new ones, has been increasing at a faster rate than have costs for any other social service—much faster than the costs of education and health.

- The money poured into prisons and keeping people in them produces very little, if any, benefits to society or our economy and, instead, drains them.

- Studies show that education is the one deterrent to crime: The more education a person has, the less likely that person will turn to crime. (16)

Stress to the public that over 80 percent of the more than 1 million in prison today are high school dropouts. They didn't or couldn't succeed in school. Each prisoner or child incarcerated costs taxpayers more than $50,000 per year (in Baltimore, according to columnist George Will [1992]), and this doesn't include the costs of property damage and personal injury and the legal fees incurred before criminals are imprisoned. Within three years, 63 percent of people who have been released commit other serious crimes and are returned to prison. It costs only $4,000 to $7,000 per year to provide a child with a public school education. Education is a good business and social investment that pays dividends to all members of society.

In Pennsylvania, it is *seven times* more expensive to keep a person in jail for four years than it is to give a full scholarship to someone attending Pennsylvania State University—and a graduate is much more likely to contribute to society. Every dollar spent on a child in the Head Start Program saves the taxpayer more than seven dollars in social services for that child later in life. According to current statistics, states with the lowest dropout rates also have the lowest number of people in prison; those with the highest dropout rates have the highest number of people in prison (Hodgkinson 1991, 14-15). So, how is the public saving money by voting down these budgets and programs?

Many myths and obstacles exist in the public mind that undermine the education of minorities:

- Learning is related to genetic heritage, and therefore whites are superior to nonwhites.

- Minorities don't want quality education and good schools.

- Education for all is a luxury; putting money into education is an expense, not an investment.

- The problems in our schools will run their course and go away.

- Every person can be a success if that person wants to be successful.

These misconceptions must be corrected.

WAYS TO COMMUNICATE

So how do we improve these communications? How do we get the message out to parents and the general public that education is succeeding much better than they think? How do we communicate to them that in order to succeed to an even greater degree and help more students, we must have certain resources and support?

First, we should focus on the positive. David Ogilvy, a well-known advertising agent says, "I spend my life speaking well of products in advertisements; I hope that you get as much pleasure out of buying them as I get out of advertising them" (1963, 2).

There are many things teachers can do to emphasize the positive:

1. Take the time to make positive phone calls to students' parents, or send positive, short notes home with the student: "John did great on his last test!" or "Peg is making a super effort to cooperate in class. I appreciate that." Ask that the note be signed by the parent(s) and returned to you. Try to call or send a note for every student in your class during the school year, maybe using a checklist to keep track. (Parents often seem befuddled, but pleasantly so, at receiving good news from school.)

2. Every two weeks or so, send home a one-page review of what your students have been studying, have accomplished, and need for school.

3. When you speak with parents or the public about school, try to do so in positive ways: what classes, projects, and students have succeeded and how others could improve. Let's tell people how many students do graduate, do go on to successful lives, and do attend regularly and exhibit good behavior. If schools are trying new approaches or programs, let's inform the public, not just parents, about why we chose to do this, what we hope to accomplish, and how it will benefit young people entering our society after they graduate from high school.

4. If someone berates education, the quality of teaching and our students, don't just agree or walk away; take the time to calmly point out the problems and what you think is needed to resolve them. Let them know that as a teacher you're just as concerned, if not more so, as they.

5. In your classroom, display slogans and buttons and even wear shirts that promote learning and education.

6. Let's deal in positive, proactive ways with radio call-in shows. Within your school, your district, your education association, enlist volunteers who will systematically phone in to local, state, and national talk-show radio. These people would present the positive side and the achievements of American students and schools as well as bring forth teacher concerns about students and schools. The district and/or education association should provide these volunteers with issue fact sheets when possible. Perhaps a community education fact sheet might be published weekly or monthly, briefly noting developments in education, learning, and what's happening with young people.

7. In the same way, let's feed the media—print, radio, and television—information about unique happenings in school, student events and accomplishments, and the teacher point of view on various issues that affect education. We could also suggest formats for television and radio programs, especially on a local and public-access level.

8. We can increase community awareness of students' work, ideas, accomplishments, thinking, and insights. Students may write essays, poems, and stories about a certain theme. Other students may draw, sculpt, or paint. Still, other young people may perform in plays and orchestras.

   The nationally known Troupe of Tellers from Roosevelt have performed for over 70,000 students in the schools and for many conferences and adult groups during the past twenty-two years; the band under Rick Wolfgang and the orchestra with David Chinburg have played in the Hult Center for the Performing Arts and repeatedly won state and regional awards; the Roosevelt Chorus has been recognized as one of the best middle school choral groups on the West Coast. The publicity and community goodwill generated by these and other student groups brings the positive public relations we need to survive and grow. Students opt to transfer to Roosevelt for its arts program, elective curriculum, and positive atmosphere. Other local high schools may repair cars, build houses, or make clothes or meals for senior citizens. Give the media information on these projects in advance and call several times as a deadline nears for them to cover what our students accomplish.

   Contact local art galleries, performing organizations, libraries, churches and synagogues, doctor and dentist offices, hospitals, shopping malls, chain stores, music and book stores, and local, state, and federal offices in the community to ask them to display student work. Check the occupations of your parents. If there are doctors, store owners, people in various organizations, contact these people so student work gets seen and appreciated.

   We should help the general public see what these students can accomplish, their perspectives of our world, and why we should value these young people so much and find an active place for them in the community.

9. Students in a class or school might publish their own newsletter for parents or for the community. This letter might contain their work, accomplishments, and feelings about local and national happenings for the general public to read.

10. The education association could organize a speakers' bureau. These teachers would be trained and available to speak to a wide range of community groups and answer questions about what's happening in schools, especially in the classroom.

11. Noneducation-oriented civic committees and organizations are a vital area in which teachers must actively participate. When we serve on the water board, the youth concerns committee, or the library board or on committees for minority affairs, human rights, or city planning, we show others that teachers are interested and committed to the entire community's welfare, not just to the school's. We establish relationships and gain insight and also learn about the power structure of the community. Others in the community then have the chance to know us as individuals with likes, dislikes, and problems similar to their own. When they do have questions about education and the schools, they know whom to contact, to listen to, and to trust.

12. Every school should develop its own component of community service and community projects as part of the school's curriculum and expectations. Students can take the responsibility to keep a community area clean, repair and paint, help care for the young or handicapped or elderly, assist in animal shelters, perform for community groups or community events, tutor, and much more. The schools should celebrate this community participation and these students' contributions both in school and publicly. (What group has worse media coverage and public image than teens? Most of this is undeserved, focusing on the small percentage of teens who do destructive acts, not on the vast majority who want to be involved and valued and to help.)

REFERENCES

Armstrong, David. 1992. *Managing by Storying Around: A New Method of Leadership*. New York: Doubleday.

Boyarsky, Steve. 1992. "U.S. Schools Doing a Good Job in Spite of Changes in Society." *Oregon Education* (December).

Bruhn, Karl. "If You're Not Part of the Solution. . . ." 1992. *NAMM News* (February): 2.

Clyde, Tom. "Your Tax Dollars at Work." 1992. *Newsweek* (June 22): 11.

Education Week. 1990. (January 14): 15.

Famous, Karen. "How to Change Education's Image—Advertise, Advertise, Advertise!" 1989. *Oregon Education* (December): 8.

Hoadley, Walter E. 1992. "What's Wrong with the Economy?" *The Commonwealth* (January 10): 39-40.

Hodgkinson, Harold. 1991. "Reform Versus Reality." *Phi Delta Kappan* (September): 9-16.

Keefer, Bob. "Neill Roan Exits Talking." 1992. *Eugene Register-Guard* (June 19): 1D.

Linkin, Larry R. "Whoelsebut. . ." 1992. *NAMM News* (February): 3.

"A Nation at Risk: The Imperative for Educational Reform: A Report to the Nation and the Secretary of Education." 1983. U.S. Department of Education, National Commission on Excellence in Education. Washington, DC: The Commission.

Ogilvy, David. *Confessions of an Advertising Man*. 1963. New York: Ballantine Books.

Rubinstein, Robert E. "Don't Kill Public Schools in the Name of 'Choice.' " 1992. *The World & I* (May): 97.

"Taxpayers: Time for a New Tea Party?" 1992. *Parade* (November 22).

What Work Requires of Schools: A SCANS Report for America 2000. 1991. Secretary's Commission on Achieving Necessary Skills. Washington, DC: U.S. Department of Labor.

Will, George. "Attention Is Main Ingredient of Program for Troubled Youths." 1992. *Eugene Register-Guard* (March 29).

12

Teaching Future Teachers to Teach

If I had my way I would turn all the teachers upside down, shake them a bit, and say: "Let's start again!" I am generalizing, obviously; of course, there are some wonderfully gifted teachers doing just what I am talking about. But unfortunately, too much of the training of teachers is based on a kind of cognitive sense of childhood, that really overlooks the experiential, perceiving kind of thing we are speaking about. Teachers by and large have become frightened of these areas.
—Richard Lewis
public school and college teacher

LACK OF EDUCATIONAL INNOVATION

Recently, a math teacher from my school took a sabbatical to work toward his masters in math. This necessitated moving to a larger city for a year to attend graduate classes in teaching math in secondary school. Several months into his sabbatical, we met and talked about his graduate school experiences. He said,

> I don't understand it. Here we are in graduate school, supposedly learning how to teach math more effectively to kids. All the professor does is lecture and assign readings. We rarely discuss issues or are allowed to voice our opinions. Most of those people in that class are teachers with a wide variety of teaching experiences. Yet, there's no time to share and learn from each other, and the professor doesn't encourage us to do so in any sense. It's difficult to get together on our own because most students commute. . . . This is not exactly a model for teaching or learning—for anyone.

The instructors and professors in colleges of education should be leading the way. They should be at the forefront of educational innovation and change, promoting positive student learning and acting as effective teachers, thus demonstrating teaching. If not, then how will our schools ever keep up with the present, much less prepare students for the future?

That this approach is, by and large, lacking in colleges is one major reason our schools have really not evolved during the past 150 years with the rest of society. Teacher trainers have, in effect, avoided promoting fundamental change in our schools by perpetuating the status quo.

One well-known professor emeritus in education I spoke with said he dropped out of the education lecture circuit because he became so discouraged with the speakers and the programs and the workshops at these education conferences. He noted that the conferences were so political, swinging to whomever or whatever was in fashion at that point, that very little new was ever accomplished. All of this, he feels, is due to the limited outlook in college education circles of people carefully working themselves up to comfortable leadership roles.

Chris Stevenson, professor at the University of Vermont, once mentioned in an April 1993 workshop the lack of actual classroom experience among those teaching in colleges of education. He observed that his sixteen years of classroom teaching represent more classroom experience than is had by all the rest of the teachers in his department combined. How can you teach about what you don't know? Where else in our society do we have people who have little or no practical experience supposedly teaching others how to do a job well?

Certainly, there are some outstanding exceptions among those teaching in education. However, very often, these educators fall into three categories: Those without any classroom experience in the public schools, those who left the public schools because they don't like teaching there or like the kids, and those who have been asked to leave the public schools. As a result, students enrolled to become future teachers will very likely endure a negative experience: They will not receive practical preparation, lack good teaching models, and will be filled with irrelevant academic information.

In turn, when these college students become our future teachers, they may convey much of this negativity in the way they relate to students because they themselves are not prepared, do not understand, and lack the necessary skills, especially interpersonal ones, to work well with young people. The young people then suffer—get turned off to education, drop out, and become behavior problems. So the cycle continues as it has done over so many years.

Stephen Glenn, in his 1991 workshop "Changing Paradigms for Youth," stated that authoritarian personalities produce three times more behavior problems with students than do nonauthoritarians and that one in four teachers acts as an authoritarian in the classroom. Thus, 25 percent of the teachers have most of the behavior problems. The personality, attitude, and personal communication skills new teachers bring to teaching are the result of the quality and type of teaching at the colleges of education.

Then, too, we have the maddening habit of trying to determine our course and development for the future by looking at our past. Many want schools to be as they were when they went to school. Educators focus narrowly on reading, writing, and math. We purposely set out, with our various national and state committees on the condition of education, to find data that fit our expectations, and we largely ignore the rest. We forget, as Stephen Glenn notes, that the national charge for education is to prepare young people to function as good citizens in our future society. Reading, writing, or math are not mentioned in the original national goal for educating students. We won't recognize that past success, based on particular values and practices, guarantees nothing with regard to future needs and values.

In April 1993, representatives of teen gangs met in Kansas City, Kansas, to discuss mutual concerns. At the meeting's conclusion, gang representatives stated that their main need was jobs and training for those jobs. (President Clinton's proposal for creating jobs for youth had, ironically, just been killed in the Senate.) These youth knew what they needed. However, their needs are not met in the public schools because quality vocational education has been eliminated or relegated to second-rate education. Their needs are also not met because colleges of education do not stress that future teachers should learn to teach vocational and personal development skills in the public schools.

RESPONSIBILITIES OF COLLEGES OF EDUCATION

What do we as teachers expect and want from colleges of education, the institutions charged with selecting, training, and inspiring future teachers to guide our children in learning and to prepare the next generation in our nation? We should hold these colleges of education responsible for making the following changes:

1. Every instructor/professor teaching classes in teacher training should:
   a. spend at least one term every three years in a school working directly with students,
   b. incorporate relevant and practical teaching applications in the classroom,
   c. model and employ a variety of teaching strategies, and
   d. be evaluated by students and peers for the quality of teaching and be held accountable for suggested improvement and growth.

2. Any student who applies to a college of education should be carefully screened at the time of entrance and during the first two years, especially for suitable personality and communication skills needed to become an effective teacher.

3. During the years students attend the teacher-training program, they should meet with an adviser several times a year, and this adviser should make notes in writing about the student's progress and any concerns with regard to that person becoming a teacher. Two times a year the adviser should observe the

student working with children, preferably in a school setting. At the end of each year, the student and adviser complete a summary of what the student has accomplished in terms of practical experiences, coursework, personal skills, and aptitude to become a teacher.

4. Every future teacher must take at least one class in either oral interpretation, beginning acting, or storytelling (not traditional speech) to improve the delivery, dynamics, and effectiveness of his or her presentations to students.

5. Every future teacher should take:
   a. an interpersonal communication class,
   b. a class on the life and times of teens today,
   c. impact training or training in another substance abuse program,
   d. a futurist and creative-thinking class, and
   e. a class in multicultural relations and values.

6. Every year, the future teacher should spend at least one term in the classroom working with students and presenting materials to groups of students. The major focus of a future teacher should be on working in the public schools with students and staff during the four- or five-year college program, not sitting in a college of education classroom.

7. A public school *teacher* and college student panel should review the course offerings and program at the college of education to help improve their effectiveness and relevance.

8. More active classroom teachers should become either visiting speakers to education classes or asked to teach classes in the colleges of education.

John Goodlad, in his book *A Place Called School* (1984), stated that until we completely restructure the methods we now use to train teachers, schools won't and can't improve. Universities and colleges give teacher training a very low priority, and future teachers learn only narrow methodologies, often by listening to lectures, rather than by practice. Goodlad proposed that teacher training take the form of medical school training: Students learn theory and put those theories into practice to see what does and does not work, and why. Such an approach stresses creative and critical thinking as well as making new discoveries.

Future teachers must carry a wide array of tools in their toolboxes, and know when and how to use them.

REFERENCES

"Are Student Teachers Better Than They Used to Be?" 1992. *NEA Today* (May): 39.

"As the Twig Is Bent. . . ." 1979. *Parabola* (November): 71.

Glenn, Stephen. "Changing Paradigms for Youth" workshop. 1991. Eugene, OR, October 11.

Goodlad, John. 1984. *A Place Called School.* New York: McGraw-Hill.

Rubinstein, Robert E. "Teacher Training: Time to Join Forces to Demand Change." 1986. *Change* (November-December): 29-30.

———. 1986. "Train Future Teachers for Role in Classroom." *Eugene Register-Guard* (January 10).

13

In the Future

---

*My greatest hope for American schools is that they pass
on love of learning and a curiosity about the world. . . .
I think an increased emphasis on our world, our problems,
and our thoughts and feelings gives children a feeling of
being connected to and compelled by their education.*
—Anna Quindlen
columnist and author

WHAT WE NEED TO KNOW

We do not know what seven out of ten jobs will be in the next century.
The average person will change careers more than five times during his or her
lifetime. So the key to education and teaching in the future is flexibility. Teachers
must change and adapt with the rapidly shifting society and world. In turn, students
must have self-confidence, knowledge, and experience with processes and technology, and creative and critical thinking skills to adapt to the societal changes. For
both students and teachers, learning will become a lifelong process.

As columnist William Raspberry (1991) stated, we must realize that there
is no one best way to improve the schools for and in the next century. School
staff, students, and parents need to work out the best and most effective ways
for their school to change. In this way, public school education will change and
improve but will do so one school at a time. School staffs must have the
confidence, time, money, and freedom to take risks, to see what unique changes
they can bring to the education of their students. We know that the best changes
in education come from the school staff, not from so-called national committees.

In all likelihood, parents will demand more choice in schools, leading to more open-enrollment policies. Public schools, in order to survive, must develop special schools. In our district, we have the International High School, a middle school devoted to computer technology, a school with a mostly elective curriculum, an opportunity center for at-risk students, a magnet arts elementary school, and language immersion schools—elementary through high school programs—in French, Spanish, and Japanese. Other districts have a similar variety of schools.

I expect that in the future, districts with several high schools will develop programs with special focuses. One school may have classes for those planning on college; another school may have an arts focus; a third may focus on applied arts and business. The key, though, is to make each program attractive with first-rate teachers, materials, and facilities that welcome students interested in taking advantage of these quality educational opportunities. We can no longer expect every high school to be able to afford to maintain caliber programs for students of widely diverse talents, needs, and interests. Special high school programs will also draw on community and business resources, on those who have a vested interest in preparing these young people.

I hope we recognize that today, and certainly in the future, the boundaries and differences between and among nations will necessarily fade as we become more socioeconomically interdependent. What happens in one part of the world will, eventually, affect everyone throughout the world in some way. So we must do much, much more to learn to understand, appreciate, and communicate with all types of peoples to ensure our survival as a planet and to have a viable future in the next century.

We must reevaluate curriculum with regard to the skills and processes students learn for the future, not in terms of what worked in the past in school. The arts, for example, which many may consider frills, are the parts of the curriculum—often the only parts—that teach critical thinking, group process, harmony, self-discipline, and interdependence and that openly encourage creativity and discovery.

Schools need to become global by networking with other schools in the country and the world. Students should employ technology to find information, knowledge, and understanding from global sources. Some schools now have become part of the Internet. Teachers, through national and global networking, can gain insight into educational and social issues, can access information, and can find new approaches.

We need to understand that most parents may be doing the best they know how under the circumstances and considering their past experiences with schools. However, the school-learning experience and environment has become like a washing machine that stops because the weight is so lopsided on the school side of the load. Many parents have, for whatever reasons, abdicated their responsibilities and now conveniently blame the school for their children's problems, characterizing schools as "bad." Today's schools have to drag the anchor of what the community perceives as past "successes" and must deal with the wide range of today's social problems. As a result, school staffs are paralyzed from being pulled in so many different directions by so many diverse special interest groups. Each group holds the schools accountable for only the school's failures, without acknowledging the school's successes. Columnist Paul Greenberg asks: "Finally, could we please stop blaming the public schools for every defect of society and everything else that may irritate us? The schools have become a kind of receiver-in-bankruptcy for the family, the churches, and society. It doesn't do much for their self-esteem" (1990, 3B).

This parent-society-school relationship simply cannot continue in this way if we hope to prepare our children for the future. We teachers must sit down with parents and explain that the responsibility for their children's learning and growth is a shared one. If parents don't support schools, don't participate in positive ways in their children's education and health, then schools cannot do the job or be held responsible for the children's learning. Parents are the key to their children's success in school. For that success to happen, parents will have to contribute much more in financing schools and as volunteers.

Teachers can and should provide the atmosphere and the opportunities for students to learn, but the students are responsible for their own learning. No one can make a student learn successfully. The values of positive attitude, working to learn and succeed, and enjoying learning still originate with and should be taught by example in the family and home. Teachers and schools cannot succeed without parental support. Alvin Toffler stated, "We need to abandon the Neanderthal notion that education takes place only in school. We all know that education is not just something that happens in our heads. It involves our total biochemistry. Neither does it occur solely within the individual. Education springs from the interplay between the individual and a changing environment."

So above all, we must understand that learning and education deal with people, life, relationships, and interpersonal communication and only secondarily with academics, facts, and figures. Our students need, more than ever, our understanding and concern for them as people, as individuals, in a chaotic, often frightening world. We, in turn, will try our best to prepare them to enter and live happily and successfully in that future world.

> But the most important way to improve schools is to have good teachers. Teachers make all the difference. Pupils either like or don't like school depending on the teachers they have. I think it should be written in a teacher's contract that he or she should be interesting, nice, loving, and caring. This is all up to teachers. (Erin K. Norby, fifth-grade student)

REFERENCES

Greenberg, Paul. 1990. "Fadtalk in Educanto Full of Junk Thought." *Eugene Register-Guard* (December 2): 3B.

"Hopes for the Future." 1991. *Instructor* (January): 78-83.

Kilpatrick, James. 1990. "2 Scholars' Educational Idea Radical." *Eugene Register-Guard* (June 18): 9A.

Raspberry, William. 1991. "Program Lets Schools Take Risks." *Eugene Register-Guard* (July 28).

Index

ABC News, 67
Abraham Maslow's Hierarchy of Needs, 26
Absenteeism, 34-35
Abused children. *See* Child abuse
Administration
    evaluation of teacher by, 126-28
    parent/teacher relationship with, 103-4
    principal's responsibilities, 124-26
    role in discipline, 51-52
    students and, 126
Adolescent changes, 21-24, 36-37
"Adolescent Crisis: The Hero's Journey," 23
Adopt a student, 40
AIDS, 28
Air circulation, 20
Alcohol abuse, 27-28, 98
Alternate-day classes, 66
America 2000, 143-44
"America's Smallest Schools: The Family," 28
Anger, 43, 135
Appreciation, 25, 38-39
Armstrong, David, 121, 122, 125
Armstrong, Thomas, 60, 77
Art
    for abused students, 57-58
    purpose of, 144
Aschbacher, Pamela, 81
Assessment. *See also* Computer, evaluations;
    Goal sheets; Grading; Group
    tests; Parent, conferences; Portfo-
    lios; Written progress reports
    communication and, 46
    personal, 2, 3
    testing as form of, 77-81
Association for Childhood Education
    International, 77
At-risk students, 34-35
    budget cuts and, 144
    dropout rates, 146
    storytelling and, 69
Attention span, 31-32, 37

Barker study, 58
Barth, Roland S., 73
Bear, Sun, 72
Behavioral changes, 21-24, 36-37
Bell curve, 81
Beyond Strength, 68
Blackboard usage, 19
Blakemore, Bill, 67
Block periods, 66
Blynt, Ruth Ann, 31
Brain
    growth, 37
    studies, 31-34
Brainstorming, 61-62
Brandeis University study, 17
Breathing exercises, 135
Bulletin boards, 18-19
Bustaque, Meg, 36
Buzan, Tony, 68

Caine, G., 33
Caine, R., 33
Cantor, Eddie, 51
Capstone questions, 83
The Carnegie Council for Adolescent
    Development, 35
Censorship, 104, 144
Chain stories, 69
"Changing Paradigms for Youth," 152
Child abuse, 98
    art and, 57-58
    statistics on, 27
Chinburg, David, 148
Cinderella, 62
Citizenship, 71-74
Class
    administration visits to, 127
    elective classes, 66
    period lengths, 123
    schedules, 66

Classroom
    atmosphere, 20, 33, 37
    Brandeis University study, 17
    bulletin boards, 18
    career experience in, 152
    decor, 8, 11, 17
    design and layout of, 19-20, 46-47
    violence, 27-28, 51-52, 137-38
Clyde, Tom, 143
College education, 153-54
"Common Miracles: The New American
        Revolution in Learning," 67
Communication
    among staff, 116-17
    Barker study, 58
    class assessment through, 46
    discipline and, 51
    negative comments in, 43, 45
    one-to-one, 46-49
    public relations and, 141
    skills for students, 122-23
    student and teacher, 45
Community
    activities, 71-74
    involvement, 53
    service, 72
Computer
    evaluations, 93
    fatigue, 137
    programs, 19
Connection classes, 123
Cooperative learning, 65-66
Coping with Job Stress, 134
Creativity
    imagery, 70
    imagination, 63
    survey, 4
    teaching, 59-63
    testing and, 80, 83
Crime, 27, 146
Cultural awareness. See Multicultural
        awareness
Curriculum
    future, 158

    material alternatives, 67
    relevancy to world, 57

deBono, Edward, 61, 122
Demonstrations, 53
Depression, 28
Desk arrangement. See Classroom,
        design and layout
The Diary of Anne Frank, 144
Diet. See Nutrition
Discipline, 50-53
Discrimination, 9-10. See also Prejudices
Divorce, 97
Dropouts, 34-35, 146
Drug abuse, 27-28, 98
Dyslexia, 34

"Early Adolescence—A Time for
        Change: Implications for
        the Family," 36
Economic Policy Institute, 142
Education
    changes in future, 157-59
    college responsibilities of, 153
    communicating success of, 147-49
    crime and, 27, 146
    dropout rates, 146
    funding for, 143-45
    informing the public about, 145-47
    innovation in, 151-53
    mutual responsibility in, 13-14
    networking in, 158
    public perceptions of, 141-42
    rules in schools, 52
    studies on, 143-44
Education Week, 142
Educational Testing Service, 28
Eitzen, D. Stanley, 27
Elective programs, 66
Ellis, Julie, 24
Ellis, Nancy, 60
Encouragement, 41
Equity Newsline, 10
Essay tests, 85-86

Evaluation. *See* Assessment; Computer, evaluations; Goal sheets; Grading; Parent, conferences; Portfolios; Written progress reports
Exercise
    job stress and, 134-35
    lack of, 28
    learning and, 57
Expression, 47, 61, 80. *See also* Creativity

Fairness, 25
Families, 97-98
Famous, Karen, 141
Farwell, David, 36
Fateful Choices, 28
Fatigue, mental, 31-32. *See also* Stress
Felible, Roma, 133
Field trips, 117
Fighting. *See* Violence
Fill-in-the-blank tests, 85
Flint, Gregory, 8
Folktales, 69
Frames of Mind, 59
"Fresh Voices," 36

Gardner, Howard, 59, 63, 80
Gavzer, Bernard, 97
Generational differences, 25-26
Glasser, William, 66
Glenn, Stephen, 2, 86, 135, 152, 153
    adopt a student, 40
    capstone questions, 83
    citizenship, 71
    creativity, 4, 62
    identity, 24
    learning, 60
    one-room schoolhouse, 34
    recall testing, 82
    suicide, 23
Goal sheets, 91
Godwin, Gail, 5
Golden, Nancy, 34
Goodlad, John, 154
Grading, 81, 89-91. *See also* Assessment; Computer, evaluations; Goal

sheets; Group tests; Parent, conferences; Portfolios; Written progress reports
Graff, Lisa, 97
Graphics, 19
Greenberg, Herbert, 134
Greenberg, Paul, 159
Gregory, Dick, 8
Grinder, Michael, 43
Group tests, 86
Gursky, Daniel, 20

Hauser, Gayelord, 134, 136
Head Start Program, 146
Hechinger, Fred M., 28
Heritage, 6, 9
Hillman, James, 63
Hoadley, Walter, 145
Hodgkinson, Harold, 142, 145-46
Hormonal changes, 36-37
Hult Center for the Performing Arts, 148
Humor, 88-89, 131-34

Illness, 28
Imagery, 70, 82
Imagination, 63, 70. *See also* Creativity; Expression
Industry Week, 133
Information
    gathering, 65
    networks, 107-8
    processing, 68
    recall, 82
Intellectual maturing, 37
Intelligences, 59-60
International High School, 158
Internet, 158
Interpersonal intelligence, 59. *See also* Intelligences
Intimacy, 35
Intimidation, 37
Intrapersonal intelligence, 59. *See also* Intelligences
IQ tests, 77, 80. *See also* Assessment; Evaluation; Grading; Testing

Jackson, Shoeless Joe, 63
Jaffe, Dennis T., 131, 135
James, Jennifer, 124
Job stress. *See* Stress

Keller, Helen, 55
Kentta, Bill, 65
"Killer phrases," 121-22
Kinesthetic intelligence, 59. *See also* Intelligences
King, Doug, 67
King, Martin Luther, Jr., 21
King, Rodney, 53
Klaulke, Amy, 58
Kushner, Malcolm, 62

Language, 13
Laughter, 131-34
Learning
  brain and, 31
  cooperative, 65-66
  disability and information, 34
  enjoyment and, 3, 57
  from each other, 55
  intelligence and, 60
  linear, 60
  logical, 60
  parents helping in, 107
  process of, 33
  skills and technology, 58-59
Lesson plan (sample), 117-18
Lighten Up: Survival Skills for People Under Pressure, 133
Lighting, 19, 20
Lincoln, Abraham, 43
Lindle, Jane C., 95, 98
Linear intelligence, 59. *See also* Intelligences
Linkin, Larry, 144
Listening, 58, 65
Littlebird, Larry, 65
Logical intelligence, 59. *See also* Intelligences
Love, 25
Luke, Bettie Sing, 80

Managing by Storying Around, 125
Marzano, Robert, 67
Masks, making, 69
Maslow, Abraham, 26
Master Teacher series (pamphlets), 116-17
Matching tests, 85
McKenzie, Jamieson, 58
Media relations, 147-48
Memory, 31-32, 68
Menninger, Karl A., 139
Mentorships, 72
Metcalf, Charles, 133
Miller, Allison, 36
Minorities
  education, obstacles of, 146-47
  perspectives of, 12
  testing and, 83
Multicultural awareness
  assessing, 11-12
  fostering, 9-12
  future world and, 57
  prejudices, 6
Multiple-choice tests, 84. *See also* Assessment; Evaluation; Grading; Testing
Multiple perspectives, 12-13
Music, 58
Musical intelligence, 59. *See also* Intelligences
Mutual responsibility, 13-14

NAEP. *See* National Assessment of Educational Progress
The Nation's At-Risk Report, 143
National Assessment of Educational Progress (NAEP), 145
National Center for Child Abuse, 27
National Education Association (NEA), 137
National education studies, 143-44
National Scholastic Survey, economic, 28
National tests, 77, 79-81
NEA. *See* National Education Association
Negative phrases, 121-22
Newsweek, 143
1990s, ins and outs of, 59
Noise, 20

Nolte, Dorothy Law, 41
Northwestern National Life Insurance
    survey, 133
Nutrition
    lack of, 28
    stress and, 136

Objectional material, 104, 144
Ogilvy, David, 147
Oldfield, David, 23
Open-note tests, 86
Oral tests, 87
Other-related teens, 24

Parade, 36, 97
Parent
    conferences, 92, 98-99, 101-3
    dealing with difficult, 104-5
    expectations, questions for, 99
    information networks for, 107-8
    night, 106-7
    role in child's behavior, 28-29, 97
    single, 97-98
    steering committees, 110
    swap day, 107
    visiting days, 107
    as volunteer, 108-10
"Parents Deserve the Blame," 97
Paul, Jordan, 113
Paul, Margaret, 113
Peers, 24
Perlman, Itzhak, 6
Perspectives, 12-13
Phi Delta Kappan, 37
Philpot, Tom, 36
Physically challenged, 6
Picture analyzation, 70
Pine, Gerald J., 8
A Place Called School, 154
Play, 25
Policy disagreements, 127-28
Pollutants, indoor, 20
Portfolios, 91
Posters, 18-19
Poverty, 28, 35
Pregnancy, 23, 27

Prejudices
    aspects of, 9-10
    assessing, 11-12
    cultural, 6
    success and, 35
Presentations in testing, 87. *See also*
    Assessment; Evaluation;
    Grading; Testing
Principals, school, 124-26
Prisons, versus education, 146
Privacy, 25
Problem students, 152
Problem solving, 60-61, 67, 122
Progress reports, written, 92-93
Projects in testing, 87. *See also* Assessment;
    Evaluation; Grading; Testing
Public education. *See* Education
Public relations, 141-49

Quindlen, Anna, 157

Racial tolerance. *See* Prejudices
Ramsey, Patricia, 11
Raspberry, William, 157
"Reach Out," 122-23
Reading teens (survey), 28-29
Recall, 68, 82
Relaxation, 138-39
Renaming students, 68
Respect, 24-26
Responsibility, 12-13, 71-74
Retention characteristics, 33. *See also*
    Memory
Ribordy, Sheila, 28
Risk-taking skills, 60-61
Rogers, Will, 57
Roosevelt Chorus, 148
Rules, 52
"Rx for Racism: Imperatives for America's
    Schools," 8

Scientific American, 45, 145
Self-awareness, 135-36
Self-defense, 137-38
Sexual activity, 27, 28
Shadow study program, 39-40

Sherry, Sylvia, 79
Short answer tests, 85-86. *See also* Assessment; Evaluation; Grading; Testing
Single-parents, 97-98
"Six-hats" problem-solving approach, 61, 122. *See also* Problem solving
Smucker, Josi, 36
Social Education, 10
Social events committee, 115
Socialization, 25
Society, today, 27-28
Sousa, David, 31
Spatial intelligence, 59. *See also* Intelligences
Speech class, 65
Sports, 28
Staff
 cohesiveness, 113-15
 conflicts of, 116-17
 meetings, 40, 119-20
Staff room settings, 115
Standardized testing report, 77, 79-81
Steering committees, 110
Stereotyping, 12
Stevenson, Chris, 57, 152
"The Sticking Place: Another Look at Grades and Grading," 31
Storytelling, 65, 69
Stress
 class schedules and, 123
 computers and, 137
 humor for, 131-34
 relaxation for, 138-39
 self-awareness for, 135-36
Stress and dyslexia, 34
Student. *See also* Teens
 administrators and, 126
 at-risk, 34-35, 69, 144
 behavioral changes in, 21-24, 35-37
 empowerment, 55
 encouragement, 41
 high/low achievement, 37
 mistakes, 36
 needing help, 46-49
 needs, 97, 100, 113
 organized demonstrations, 53

 parent/teacher support, 106-7
 self-confidence, 122-23
 siblings and, 38
 staff meetings focusing on, 119-20
 success, obstacles to, 35
 tricks, 36
 trust from teachers, 38
 workshops, 53
Substitute teachers, 117-18
Suicide, 23, 27, 28, 90

Tales, 69
Teacher
 administrator relationship with, 126-28
 as adviser, 51
 appreciation/trust of student, 38-39
 attitude, 38
 change and, 121-24
 evaluation of, 126-28
 future of the, 151-53
 harmful/helpful behaviors of, 6
 parent relationship with, 92, 98-99, 102-4
 personal assessment, 2, 3
 preparation and student success, 37
 principal relationship with, 124-26
 public perception of, 142
 responsibility of, 5
 self-defense for, 137-38
 training, 154
Teacher Magazine, 20
Teaching
 anger and, 43
 attributes, 3
 change in, 121-24
 difficult parents and, 103-5
 future evolution of, 157-59
 general approach 1, 2
 job stress and, 131-39
 material alternatives, 67
 parental expectations of, 98-100
 for specific tests, 83
 style assessment, 3
 what and how, 63, 66-67

Teaching and Learning in a Diverse World, 11
Technology, 58-59
Teens. *See also* Students
  at-risk, 34-35, 69, 143-44
  contemporary life of, 21-24
  generational differences, 25-26
  needs, 26
  peers and, 24
  pregnancy, 23, 27
  reading by, 28-29
  respecting, 24-26
  sexual activity, 27, 28
  suicide, 23, 27, 28, 90
  in transition, 24, 35
Television, 28-29
Telling tales, 69
Testing. *See also* Assessment;
    Evaluation; Grading
  as assessment, 77-81
  bias of, 81, 83
  brain and, 33
  cheating, 89
  costs, 81
  creating, 82-83
  essay, 85-86
  fill-in-the-blanks, 85
  group, 86
  help during, 89
  humor and, 88-89
  imagery and, 82
  interviews, 88
  matching, 85
  multiple-choice, 84
  open-note, 86
  oral, 87
  preparation for, 81-82
  projects or presentations in, 87-88
  reviewing with student, 90
  scoring, 89
  short answer, 85-86
  specific, 83-88
  student-centered approach, 79
  student-created, 87

timed, 83
true-or-false, 84
Thinking skills
  brain and, 31
  creativity and, 60
  developing, 59-63
  higher-order, 67
Toffler, Alvin, 159
Tradition, 21-24
Troupe of Tellers (storytelling troupe),
    148
Truancy, 34-35, 146
Truths, 12

"Understanding a Brain-Based Ap-
    proach to Learning and
    Teaching," 33
U.S. Bureau of Census, teens in crisis, 28
U.S. Bureau of Labor Statistics, 10

Violence
  in classroom, 51-52, 137-38
  societal, 27-28
Visiting days, 107
Visualization, 68, 82, 135-36
Volunteers, 108
  projects for teens, 73-74
  resource questionnaire for, 109
von Oech, Roger, 49, 67

"What Is a Family?" 97
White-Hood, Marian, 9, 24
Will, George, 146
Windows, 124
Wolfgang, Rick, 148
Workshops, 53
Writing, studies on, 58
Written progress reports, 92-93. *See also*
    Assessment; Evaluation;
    Grading; Testing
Written tests, 83. *See also* Assessment;
    Evaluation; Grading; Testing

About the Author

For the past twenty-five years, Robert Rubinstein has been a teacher of language arts and performing arts at the junior high and middle school level. He received his teaching credential from the University of Oregon, a master's degree in English from Northeastern University, and a master's degree in journalism from the University of Oregon. He is also a professional storyteller and writer.

At Roosevelt Middle School in Eugene, Oregon, he has originated, designed, organized, and taught more than thirty elective classes, ranging from storytelling, reader's theatre, and monsters to medieval history, word games, and sports history, for both low- and high-skilled students. For the Eugene Education Association,

he developed and chaired the first "How to Help Your Child Learn Night" for parents. In spring 1986, the Oregon Education Association awarded him the Noel Connall Instructional Professional Development Award.

Rubinstein founded and is director of the nationally-known Troupe of Tellers from Roosevelt Middle School. Since 1969, these troupes, composed of sixth-through eighth-grade students, have performed for more than 70,000 students in elementary schools and for civic and educational groups. Robert Rubinstein has recorded three storytelling tapes, including *The Rooster Who Would Be King and Other Healing Tales*, which received a *Parents' Choice* "Seal of Approval."

Rubinstein has written two young adult novels: *Who Wants to Be a Hero!* and *When Sirens Scream*. *Hero* was made into a television film for Showtime. In 1983, *Sirens* was named by ALA's *Booklist* as a notable young adult novel on the issue of nuclear power. Rubinstein is also the author of numerous articles appearing in national and regional publications.

Robert Rubinstein lives in Eugene with his wife, three teenage children, and Kira, a hyperactive border collie.